Money Minded Families

Money Minded Families

How to Raise Financially Well Children

Stephanie W. Mackara

WILEY

For general information on our other products and services or for technical support, please contact our Customer Care Department within the United States at (800) 762–2974, outside the United States at (317) 572–3993, or fax (317) 572–4002.

Wiley publishes in a variety of print and electronic formats and by print-on-demand. Some material included with standard print versions of this book may not be included in e-books or in print-on-demand. If this book refers to media such as a CD or DVD that is not included in the version you purchased, you may download this material at http://booksupport.wiley.com. For more information about Wiley products, visit www.wiley.com.

Library of Congress Cataloging-in-Publication Data is Available:

9781119635901 (Hardback)
9781119636021 (ePDF)
9781119636007 (epub).

Cover Design: Wiley
Cover Image: © Sara Shrouds of Abstract Sara Studios

Printed in the United States of America

V10018065_031620

To Bernie
For hearing my thoughts, understanding my dreams, and being my best friend...
For filling my life with music, and loving me without end... thank you.

Contents

Acknowledgments

Writing a book is harder than I thought and more rewarding than I could have ever imagined. None of this would have been possible without the love, support and inspiration from my boys Bernie and Jacob. Bernie for giving me the space and encouragement to follow my passions and Jacob for being my guinea pig, my heart and my inspiration.

I'm eternally grateful to all of amazing colleagues I have the pleasure of calling my friends over my career who have led, empowered and showed me that anything is possible. I learned so much about business, leadership and grace from each of you.

To my girls, my chosen family, whose unwavering support, compassion and honesty I cherish. To my Mom, brother Michael and sister Karen, who helped to guide and shape my experiences and my person as I grew, these memories and experiences led me here.

To everyone at Wiley for taking a chance on me and my book. Thank you for turning my scribbles into something more.

Finally, a huge THANK YOU! to all the others who encouraged me along this journey and have been a part of making this dream come true.

Introduction

In addition to being chefs, therapists, nurses, chauffeurs, and more, parents are inevitably teachers, despite most of us not having a degree in education (or for that matter, in any of these professions). For so many facets of parenthood, there is no guidebook or instruction manual. As parents, we tend to focus most of our energies on the emotional and physical wellbeing of our children. I propose we must also focus on their financial wellbeing.

Children are extraordinary learners from a very young age. They master concepts, language, walking, negotiating, and more in just their first few years. Yet we typically don't engage our children in learning about financial matters until much later in life, if ever. This is a mistake. In fact, perhaps because of this mistake, many parents never truly become knowledgeable about basic finances, let alone master their own.

According to the Consumer Financial Protection Bureau, "financial wellbeing" is defined as "a state of being wherein you have control over day-to-day, month-to-month finances; have the capacity to absorb a financial shock; are on track to meet your financial goals; and have the financial freedom to make the choices that allow you to enjoy life." My definition of financial wellbeing is much simpler. Financial wellbeing is a state of clarity, purpose, and direction; it is not separate from your personal wellbeing, in fact, *financial wellbeing is inextricably intertwined with your overall health*. We must begin to incorporate all aspects of wellbeing into our daily lives: emotional, physical, and financial, in order to optimize our personal health. And it must begin at a very young age.

As someone with a career in finance, I want to help you have important conversations and experiences about money with your children. Recognizing and making the most of "teachable moments" as they present themselves can help shape your children's future attitudes and behavior around their finances and give them a sense of financial wellbeing. After all, parenting is, if nothing else, teaching our children to make smart choices that allow them to enjoy life.

I have a son of my own, Jacob. My husband, Bernie, and I have worked hard to lay the groundwork to help him create smart and healthy financial habits. Starting when he played with a toy cash register as a toddler, I tried to teach him how credit cards work. He was too young to fully grasp the lesson then, but our conversations about money evolve as he grows up. I wish I had the same open communication with my own parents when I was a kid. Instead, I grew up like many children of my generation where money was a taboo topic in our house. When I asked my parents about their salaries, I was told I was being crass and inappropriate. It made me feel that money was bad, something never to discuss. It took me years to correct this negative association. Never forgetting how that made me feel, I want to make sure that Jacob knows only open and honest communication about money that helps him build the foundation of a successful and healthy relationship with his own finances and in his life.

This is not to judge my parents' parenting. As parents, we are all often just treading water, doing the very best we can. But I do think we need to pay attention, listen closely, and be present when it comes to talking about money and finances. Our kids so desperately need guidance. I encourage you not to underestimate the people and lessons in your children's lives and the permanent impact they can have on their financial behaviors, attitudes, and overall wellbeing. I was fortunate to have close friends throughout high school and college who were taught basic financial concepts and did offer guidance that intrigued me—so much so that I wanted to learn and understand more about how best to earn, invest, and spend money. Maybe this is what led me to my current profession as a financial advisor.

As parents, we must prioritize teaching our children smart financial habits while attributing positive connections with money. Today's technological landscape has made teaching kids about money increasingly difficult. Consider that the way most of us were introduced to money was with actual dollars in hand. We walked into a store, picked out what we wanted, and had to figure out how many of those dollars to hand over. Today, children have gift cards, online shopping, and apps for purchases and as a result they can go years without ever really handling money other than play money from that toy cash register.

We so often hear the word "entitled" to describe kids today. I personally think the word is overused and incorrectly applied, except when it comes to the expectations children have about getting things—then it's right on point. The question is: Why do our kids feel so entitled? Why do they feel as though they have the right to simply "get" everything they want simply because they want it?

The answer is that the culture we live in, and many of us, have fed into this environment of instant gratification for our children, and unless we figure out how to break the cycle of expectation, we will set our kids up for failure as adults, particularly when it comes to their becoming financially independent and successful. So, let's stop blaming our kids for their sense of entitlement and do something about it. Melinda Gates, who has more money than most of us can ever dream of, recently said about raising her children that she could never say "No, you can't have that item because we can't afford it"; what she did instead was help her children understand that just because you can afford something doesn't mean that you should buy it.

When I was in college, only a lucky few had parents who paid for all their college costs and expenses. Today, for many, parents paying for college is an expectation. In fact, not only are we paying, but we start planning for these costs when our kids are right out of the womb. Many people save more for their children's college than their own retirement. I'm not suggesting we shouldn't plan for our children's future. Bernie and I are in fact saving aggressively for my son's college education. As a mom, like most, I want the best possible future for my son, and I know a college degree will push him toward his future earning potential. However, we want him to understand the value of that degree, our expectations of him, as well as the cost of each class and each missed class. We try hard to reinforce that we will help him because, through his hard work in school and sports, and as a good friend and community contributor, he has earned our support; there is no free lunch. *Earned* is the operative word.

When I think of the struggles of raising children to be financially competent adults, I think of the Chinese proverb: "Give a man a fish, and you feed him for a day. Teach a man to fish, and you feed him for a lifetime."

Feeding all of your child's financial wants day in and day out can create a cycle of dependency and a lack of resourcefulness on the part of your child. I hope after reading this book you can teach your children how to feed their own financial needs and wants and ultimately set them on a successful path toward their own financial wellbeing. I also hope this book will help adults who may not have a healthy relationship with money to reflect on the reasons behind their own financial habits and begin to live a life of financial wellness.

I'd like this book to be used as a tool to help you guide your children, and to be shared with your children. The goal is to help raise strong, educated people who have the know-how and desire to set and achieve financial goals for themselves, save and spend with clarity, and understand the value and purpose of their work and of material things. We do this by understanding and perhaps redefining our own money personalities and working to create positive financial socialization for our children.

What this book is *not* is a prescription telling you exactly what to do. I firmly believe there is no one way to parent and particularly to help children engage with money in a positive way. Each family and each child within the family is unique. My hope is that you and your family will find the path that works best for you. Throughout this book you'll find lots of studies, data, and numbers (it *is* a book on finance after all), but perhaps even more importantly, you'll find examples of how to talk to your children about money and why these conversations are crucial to their financial wellbeing. I'm sharing not only lessons I've learned from my career in finance, but my own money mistakes and lessons learned so you can teach your sons and daughters how to "fish" and become financially prepared for adult life.

Journalist Sydney J. Harris made the brilliant analogy that "the whole purpose of education is to turn mirrors into windows. When you gaze into a mirror, the only things you see are your reflection and a limited area around you. However, when you look out a window, the view can be almost endless." Helping educate yourself and your children about their behaviors toward finance will, without a doubt, have a dramatic change on their view of money, seeing it as a tool offering endless possibilities and helping to enrich their quality of life as it relates to their financial wellbeing.

1

Background: A Little Bit of "Retirement" History

Developing a healthy relationship with money and finances is a lifelong journey. That journey starts at young toddler age, extends throughout your entire life, and has ramifications at each step, all the way to the handling and distribution of your estate after you are deceased. Yet in this country we are generally fixated on one and only one step or destination, rather than on the journey. That destination is what we have labeled *retirement*. In this book, my goal is to give you and your family tools to manage your finances and goals throughout the journey, with the understanding that our children are being raised in a very different time, one in which "retirement" must be redefined or simply dismissed as the "goal." I thought it prudent to provide a quick history of how retirement came to be and how it must change for future generations.

In the late 1800s, when the concept of retirement as a government policy was adopted first in Germany under Otto Von Bismarck, "retirement" at that time had a very different meaning. Bismarck introduced the idea of retirement as a modern government pension, a financial benefit for workers once they reached the age of 70 and most could no longer perform physical work. Before this concept, if you lived, you worked; there was no stopping or retiring from one's job. Otto wasn't motivated by compassion for the plight of the working class, but rather wanted to preempt a growing socialist movement in Germany before it grew any more powerful, and therefore provide the people of Germany with financial support, something they couldn't manage on their own and would keep the people happy with his leadership. This new pension provided government financial support to the aging population in Germany and was the first time in history people began to *plan* to retire (*Source:* https://www.theatlantic.com/business/archive/2014/10/how-retirement-was-invented/381802/).

This idea of working to live quickly changed and people across the globe became enamored with the idea that they could stop working at a certain age, and with the financial support of the government live out their last few years of life taking it easy. As evidenced by the labor force participation rates, "retirement" as we know it today is a twentieth-century phenomenon. People in the late 1800s and early 1900s had shorter life expectancies and typically ran their family farms for most of their adult lives. The rich managed their estates. No matter their status, most continued to work until they died. Consider that in 1880, the labor participation rate of men age 65 and older was 78%. However, through the beginning of this century, the participation rate of men over 65 in the workforce has steadily and dramatically declined. (In 2000 the rate was just 18.4%!)

Retirement became a natural expectation and has come to be viewed, ideally, as an extended period of independence and leisure. So, what has changed? A lot; the shift from agriculture to industry had a significant impact on how people worked. No one truly retired from an agriculture position. That agricultural work was typically not just a way to earn money, but a way to live and have a home. As evidenced in many early wills prior to the twentieth century, a "retirement plan" entailed having as many children as possible so that, in exchange for the house and farm, the children would care for their elder parents in their final years of life.

With the Industrial Revolution, younger generations were able to leave the home to find different types of work and increase their standards of living. This generation entering the workplace created a shift from people having children as a plan for caretaking in retirement to having bank accounts. As children no longer stayed at home, elders could no longer rely on their children to care for them in retirement as they aged, so we also saw a decrease in the number of children being born and coupled with an increase in savings rates.

With the Industrial Revolution also came the five-day workweek, something unheard of in agriculture. To keep workers happy, employers started providing benefits in the form of pensions or other defined benefits that employees would collect only after decades of service. American Express offered its first pension as early as 1875 in order to entice workers to join the company. These defined benefits were "guaranteed" specific dollar amounts to be received each month, funded and paid entirely by the employer if you worked for the company until, say, age 65. Age 65 was seen as "old age"; there were studies that showed a mental and physical decline in workers over the age of 60 and so 65 became known as the target when one should retire. We quickly shifted from working to live to working to retire.

Enter Franklin Delano Roosevelt's first rendition of Social Security on August 14, 1935. The purpose was to provide public pensions to those not covered by private pensions. Social Security was paid into by most employees via a tax from their paychecks and a "pension" payment was made at full retirement age, which (at the time) 65. Taxes to fund Social Security first started being collected in January 1937 and the first benefit payment was paid in 1940. Today, Social Security has morphed and expanded significantly from its original form (more on that later).

Another important, and probably the most critical factor in our view of retirement today, is the marked and continual increase in Americans' standard of living during the Industrial Revolution through today. Today, Americans enjoy a standard of living commensurate with eight times the average American income of a century ago. The rise in opportunity, income, and increased savings rates has provided many the opportunity to spend time and money on things previously only available to the wealthy. Additionally, global industry has decreased the costs of many goods previously considered luxury items.

In 1803, the economist John Baptiste Say explained what is now called "Say's law," which states, "It is worthwhile to remark that a product is no sooner created than it, from that instant, affords a market for other products to the full extent of its own value" (*Source:* J. B. Say, *A Treatise on Political Economy*, 1803, pp.138–139). In other words, supply creates its own demand.

At no time in history was this more accurate. Industry was creating more and more goods at affordable prices and, for the first time, private companies or government were funding decades of work-free years. As a result, masses of Americans had extra time and money to spend. This is how today's ideal vision of retirement came to be. This created an environment where savers and spenders both were in a good financial position. The only difference was how much money was left to their children at the time of their passing. Big savers didn't have to spend much, if any, of their own savings on retirement simply because the access to the other financial resources was enough to cover their spending while spenders continued to spend because the government was paying for it!.

The children who may have been left an inheritance from these savers are the current generation of Boomers, and guess what they did? According to Dr. Jay Zagorsky, senior lecturer at Boston University Questrom School of Business, one out of three Baby Boomers who received an inheritance spent it within two years. The good savings habits of their parents somehow did not pass forward to these future generations. Why? I am not certain, but it could have a lot to do with the lack of communication many families have about financial matters. It's time to change that.

Consider families today. Most don't wait until retirement to take a wonderful vacation or to buy the house of their dreams; they buy it when they desire it. We have increased our spending habits but our resources to fund retirement have not been replenished. This has mass implications on many people's retirement savings and more drastically the ability to realize retirement as a destination at all. As you read through this book, it is important to understand how our financial world was formed and how it has changed, quite dramatically, in order to fully appreciate our roles and the need to make a change for our children's future—one that could very likely not include a true period of retirement as we know it today.

2

The Current State of "Retirement"

When people first started "retirement planning," their focus was often on what was known as a three-legged stool. Each leg of the stool represented a foundation of financial support to count on during retirement, removing the fear of outliving personal resources. The three legs were employer-defined benefit plans or pensions, Social Security, and personal savings. The personal savings leg of the stool was typically used to fund the proverbial "bucket list" while the Social Security and pension supported most people's day-to-day living expenses.

Retirement planning forecasts were then filled with excellent news. We had great "pensions"; many committed to paying private or federal employees the average of their top-three working years for the rest of their lives! They were getting paid the same amount in retirement as in their top-earning years; a lucky few have actually earned more in retirement than in their working years! The government provided Social Security, incomes were growing, access to more luxury items was available, and most people were working fewer years so that they could enjoy all the wonderful bounty! Life was great.

But things have changed for most Americans.

In the previous chapter, we discussed the dramatic decline in the labor force for men age 65 and older at the beginning of this century. What do you think has happened since then? We have seen a marked *increase* in the labor participation rates of older men, and women, too. In 2009, more than 36% of men ages 65–69 were actively engaged in the workforce. Remember this same participation rate was only 18.4% in 2000. These numbers have similarly increased for men age 70 and older (*Source: Older Adults' Labor Force Participation since 1993: A Decade and a Half of Growth*, January 2010, Richard W. Johnson and James Kaminski).

Why have Americans started working into what just a few years ago we considered "retirement"? There are many reasons of course. To start, wages have become stagnant, and healthcare and education costs have increased *astronomically*. Combine this with the disappearance of most private pension systems and a broken Social Security system, and we now have an environment where "retirement" is an elusive concept. Increased personal and national debt also continue to eat away at our ability to both save and invest.

Remember how generous American Express was in 1875, offering the first private pension for their retired employees? In 2009 they decided it was simply unsustainable and stopped offering these generous pensions. American Express is not unlike many other corporations that simply can no longer afford to pay pensions to their employees. Instead, most have replaced traditional pensions and defined benefits with defined-contribution or what most of us know as 401(k) plans. These plans require employees to save their own money for retirement. This ends up morphing two of the three legs of the retirement stool together, creating a great imbalance toward your personal savings.

Consider how much a household needs to spend during their retirement years. For those who entered retirement in the 1970s, the typical income replacement rate was about 65% of pre-retirement income, meaning, if you earned $100,000 a year, you would expect to need $65,000 each year in retirement to maintain your current lifestyle. The $65,000 was covered by those three legs of the stool: Social Security, private pension/retirement plan, and personal savings—mostly, if not all, the Social Security and private pensions.

Using the three-legged-stool example made it easy to understand how much you would need to save for retirement because two of the three legs were static and easily quantifiable. That is, you knew if you retired at 65, you would receive a fixed amount per month in Social Security and a fixed amount per month in pension. These figures may have grown slightly with inflation, but for the most part these were fixed figures. Most individuals entering retirement had little to no debt, so their day-to-day expenses were relatively low as compared to their pre-retirement needs. The only variable was what you contributed toward you own retirement income. For a great number of people, pension and/or Social Security was enough to cover everything.

Today, the three-legged stool has lost two legs and can barely support retirement income needs. Most companies are no longer providing pensions, or the pensions are insolvent. A July 30, 2018, *Wall Street Journal* article cites that the pension hole or deficit owed to employees for US cities and states is the size of Germany's entire economy. Pause here for a moment. Take that in: the deficit owed to US city employees is the size of Germany, the fourth-largest economy (ranked by GDP) in the world! This is just an enormous debt that continues to grow every day. Social Security has been modified over time and is not sustainable at its current levels. The latest report from the Social Security and Medicare Board of Trustees (as of 2018) suggests that in 2034, Social Security will only be able to pay out at 77% of retirees' benefits and those benefits will be starting later and later in life. Like city pensions, the Social Security commitments continue to grow and, as a country, we continue to brush aside the enormity of the issue. The answers aren't easy, but they are doable with strong leadership. We either cut benefits, increase the benefit age, increase taxes, or borrow from somewhere else in the government to fund the deficit. Each of these has been discussed, but never implemented because, politically, the solutions aren't popular. As a result, here we sit, waiting and watching for it to blow up, not clear when it will happen or who will get this third leg of the stool pulled out from beneath them.

So, today, most of us are left with one source of retirement savings—ourselves. Not only have two stool legs of support been removed, but our planning must now replace 80% of our pre-retirement income because we are living longer, healthcare is more expensive, and our personal debt—either by way of mortgages or student loans for ourselves or our children—tends to stay with us a great deal longer and often into retirement.

One of the greatest financial accounts created was the 401(k), or the defined-contribution plan. As we previously discussed, this was created to replace many corporate private pensions and allow individuals to save pre-tax dollars toward their retirement. What most people don't know is that it was never created to be the main source of employee retirement savings it is today. The accidental retirement revolution began in 1978 when Congress passed the Revenue Act of 1978. The Act included a provision, Section 401(k), that gave employees a tax-free way to take money from bonuses or stock options and save without paying taxes, deferring them to some future date. A gentleman named Ted Benna, a benefits consultant at the Johnson Companies, is today regarded as the father of the 401(k). When working with a client who wanted to provide benefits to its employees and also incentivize its employees to save, Ted Benna advised that the new Section 401(k) of the Revenue Act of 1978 could be the solution they needed. There wasn't anything explicit or hidden in the code that said the modern version of the 401(k) could be used as an Employer Deferred Compensation Plan, but there also wasn't anything in the code that said it couldn't. Through some creativity and a bit of a fluke in helping his client, Ted Benna created the first 401(k) plan.

Based on Benna's work, in 1981 the IRS issued rules that allowed employees to contribute to accounts through salary deductions; this created efficiency and scale and jumpstarted the widespread rollout of the plans in the early 1980s (*Source: 401(k)—Forty Years Later*, Ted Benna).

There was a great deal of concern that pensions would go away, and in fact they did, not because of the 401(k), but in spite of it. In just a few short years from its creation, large companies began to offer the 401(k) plans, mainly because it was less expensive than funding pensions and was more predictable to fund. Over the years the contribution amounts an employee is able to save through deferral have increased, including a catch-up contribution for those over 50. Starting in 2020, the total employee deferral can be up to $19,500 with a catch-up of $6,500; so those over 50 can put as much as $26,000 into their 401(k) accounts.

Many companies not only provide the 401(k) plan, they also match or contribute 4% or more of the employee's savings. For instance, for an employee earning $50,000, if the employee participates in the plan, most employers will offer to match the first 3% of their salary deferral amounts and then 50% up to 5%. Confusing, but simply, if the employee defers 5% of their salary toward the 401(k), the employer gives them 4% of their salary in savings—we call this free money! In total the employee is now saving 9% or $4,500 a year.

This is a great way to start saving, but it cannot be the only place one saves toward retirement. In the above example, savings of 5% with a company match earning $50,000 over 35 years with a 6% return will get you approximately $538,000 to use for retirement income. This is a nice nest egg, but if it is your only leg of the stool, it most likely can't sustain your entire retirement income needs. Instead, save more, save early, and save often (more on that later).

As I write this, I am a 45-year-old financial advisor. As a financial advisor, I see that even many educated people with great means are not in control of their own financial situations and their spending, and savings are not on track to being able to retire comfortably. This could be because we as a nation simply have not focused on teaching the basics of becoming financially healthy—honestly, because most of us never had to. Now, as I look to the future, I fear not as much for my mom or her peers, or even for myself, but for my son and his friends, cousins, and peers— for our children and the next generation. Today we are faced with an unprecedented culmination of events. As a nation, we are woefully unprepared for the effects this will have on our schools and communities. The three-legged stool has been flipped on its head by a three-headed monster:

- Personal debt or consumer debt is at $13.86 trillion, primarily school loans, which are second only to mortgage debt.
- National debt: according to the *New York Times* just the interest payments on the US national debt will overtake Medicaid costs in 2020 and the Department of Defense budget in 2023.
- Decreased corporate and government support for retirement: in 2018, for the first time since 1982, Social Security will pay out more than it takes in, with a projected date to run out by 2034.

Our country's financial foundation is no longer stable and the only way to fix it for ourselves and future generations is to take charge and DIY (do it yourself). The financial changes our country is faced with make it so important for us to shift our thinking from allowing our children to take minimal personal responsibility and acquire limited financial knowledge, to consciously increasing the level of education our children receive relative to financial matters. The next few generations don't have the luxury of waiting until age 50 or 60 to pay attention to their financial wellness and money management habits.

With so many factors beyond our control and so many new financial complexities offered as solutions—such as investment products and potential debt offerings solutions—taking financial control can feel completely overwhelming. Yet instead of burying our heads in the sand and wishing, hoping, and maybe praying that someone or something will solve the financial puzzle for us, we must take control. We cannot rely on government or private corporations so we must grab the bull by the horns and take it for a ride. The silver lining is that by creating good habits and being disciplined, you can succeed at becoming financially well. By starting your children off with positive financial habits at a young age, you'll help them have a greater chance of absorbing and implementing those habits in their adult lives. Learning to save, spend, share, and invest wisely, along with positive financial socialization and a positive relationship with money, are the key ingredients to your personal (and your child's) financial wellness and future retirement.

There is a movement that started that you may have heard of called FIRE. It stands for Financially Independent Retire Early. This movement was led by a Canadian named Peter Adeney, whose pseudonym, Mr. Money Moustache, has a cult-like following. He retired at the age of 30 and shares his wisdom with others to help them do the same. There are lots of naysayers about the FIRE movement. The two biggest gripes I have heard is that the group tends to make work sound bad and the sooner you can stop working the better, and that it's practices require extreme frugality. Though participants within the FIRE movement tend to be more frugal than most, the group is made up of all different kinds of people in many different circumstances and in fact, though Mr. MM started the trend, there are now many different factions. And, about the "not working" concept—this isn't at all what the movement is about; it's about being financially independent. Financial independence doesn't mean the end of a working career. In the words of Mr. Money Moustache himself, it means "complete freedom to be the best, most powerful, energetic, happiest, and most generous version of You that you can possibly be."

This movement isn't for everyone; in fact many find it to be too constricting in terms of spending. I am lucky enough to be in a few groups with people who are part of the FIRE movement and what I most enjoy about them is they all come from different backgrounds, with different experiences, but they are all very curious and active when it comes to making smart financial decisions and they are always, always willing to share and support and celebrate each other. Being frugal used to be labeled as depriving yourself; this group has turned being thrifty into liberation. Though not for everyone, its mere existence is evidence that we as a society are taking the bull by the horns and developing strategies to make sure one can be financially independent and not rely on a government or a corporation to dictate when and what our retirement will look like. Though my lifestyle isn't perfectly aligned with the FIRE movement, the message it sends is one I can get behind. We control our financial destiny and as a result must be a mindful, active participant.

So, what will the big *R* look like for our children? Will we return to the preindustrial age where retirement didn't even exist or will only be available to the 1% as a luxury? Or will we find new and different ways to earn money, spend money, and save money? Will there be new ways to age, new algorithms to better plan for retirement, new government or social supports to fund our lifestyle once we stop working? Will we change the way we work, searching for purpose instead of a paycheck? Will there be stages to our "end of working years"? All of this is unknown, but what we do know is that technology will surely make it easier to continue to earn money in ways we haven't even considered today—in ways that may incur less stress or physical burden on our bodies, much of the reason people stop working today. Will the idea of retirement change completely? Perhaps, but no matter the changes, our children will still need a strong financial foundation in order to help them live their best lives.

We are facing a great burden for our children, one that none of us have experience with, but one that we must prepare for. I have great hope that educating our children on matters of both financial wellness and financial literacy while preparing them for the burden that lies ahead will allow them to change the tenor of their future and of future generations. There is so much to fix, but it *is* fixable. There is much work to be done and we as parents are privileged to help our children get it done.

3

Financial Socialization: Creating Spending, Budgeting, and Saving Habits

How will our children learn to navigate these treacherous new waters without an experienced guide? Just like traveling in a new city, they will figure it out, preferably with your help. There may be a few twists and wrong turns, but ultimately, with focus and presence of mind, our children will find their way to being financially well—if not, they will be forever lost. Consider our children's spending habits today.

Do you remember when Amazon only sold books? I sure do! On August 5, 1998, "Amazon.com Is Expanding Beyond Books" was a *New York Times* headline. The article reported that "Amazon.com has grown to be the most successful merchant on the Internet, with 3.1 million customers." Today Amazon has more than 310 million active customers and sells more than 12 million products, not including books (*Source:* Number of Active Amazon Customer Accounts Worldwide, Statista, and How Many Products Does Amazon Carry?, Retail Touchpoints).

Amazon and a seemingly infinite number of online shopping sites have given us unprecedented access to goods and services—and ways to spend money. Subsequently, that access has helped us create a culture of instant gratification and excess. Increased consumption and a stable labor market have led to greater spending in the United States, which may be a good sign for our economy, but this type of access to goods has both changed the way we spend and created a culture of excess. The technology behind consumerism is evolving at such a fast rate that it is difficult to fathom what will be next. While these changes to consumerism did not come with an instruction manual, it is clear that instant access and excess are not conducive to helping us become financially well. It is a whole new world, but we must meet our children where they are and understand the daily challenges they face.

The Consumer Financial Health Study (Center for Financial Services Innovation, March 2015, https://s3.amazonaws.com/cfsi-innovation-files/wp-content/uploads/2017/01/24183123/Understanding-and-Improving-Consumer-Financial-Health-in-America.pdf) finds that not only are 57% of Americans "financially unhealthy," but 26% say their finances cause them significant stress, 43% struggle to keep up with bills, and 36% are not confident they could come up with $2,000 in the next month if an emergency arose. So, we are now entirely responsible for our financial resources in retirement, but the majority of Americans are struggling to keep up with their daily finances, even before they can consider saving for retirement. This, too, is a new challenge.

As Americans we must become more conscious of our financial journey before, during, and after retirement. We must work toward living a life of financial mindfulness and wellbeing in order to better enjoy our present lives as well as our future retirements. The words of Arthur Ashe echo in my mind: "Success is a journey, not a destination. The doing is often more important than the outcome."

Now comes the good news. Financial wellbeing can be learned and practiced, like any other life skill. Spending, managing cash flow and credit, and saving and investing practices all influence financial wellbeing—for better or for worse. So how do we create spending, saving, and investment practices that have a positive effect on our financial wellbeing?

Consider that 30 to 40% of retirement wealth inequality can be accounted for by "financial knowledge" (*Source:* "Optimal Financial Knowledge and Wealth Inequality," Annamaria Lusardi, Pierre-Carl Michaud, and Olivia S. Mitchell, 2017, *Journal of Political Economy*, vol. 125(2), University of Chicago Press, pp. 431–477). That 30 to 40% can make the difference between living on a fixed budget versus enjoying the life of leisure, meaning, and purpose that each of us has always dreamed about.

So, what is the best way to acquire this financial knowledge? For our children, it's positive "financial socialization." Financial socialization is the process by which young people acquire the standards, values, norms, skills, knowledge, and attitudes needed to become functioning consumers in the marketplace (*Source: Journal of Financial Counseling and Planning*, 2013). It is a learned process of acquiring knowledge about money and developing skills such as banking, budgeting, saving, spending, investing, and using credit cards.

Financial socialization is the way most people learn how to handle their financial affairs. Who do you think are their primary teachers? You got it: parents. Every hour of every day, parents are "teaching" their children about finances, among many other things, with their own behavior. If you make a habit of spending unconsciously or irresponsibly, you run the risk not only of creating your own negative financial situation, but also of passing your financially unhealthy behavior onto your children.

Two separate studies about parental influence on children (B. L. Jorgensen and J. Savla, 2010, "Financial Literacy of Young Adults: The Importance of Parental Socialization," *Family Relations*, 59(4), 465–478, and Clinton Gudmunson and Sharon Danes, 2011, "Family Financial Socialization: Theory and Critical Review,"

Journal of Family and Economic Issues, Springer, vol. 32(4), pp. 644–667, December) confirmed that parental influence through financial socialization has a "direct and significant" influence on the attitudes and financial behavior of children and young adults. The findings of these and many other studies, coupled with the poor state of financial affairs in the United States our children will inherit, has prompted US government and many US nonprofits to focus on helping improve our children's financial literacy. Despite the importance of these efforts, research consistently shows that, like most learned behaviors, family and the dynamics within families have the strongest influence on children's financial knowledge (*Source:* Shim et al., *Financial Socialization of First-Year College Students: The Roles of Parents, Work, and Education,* 2009, 2010, https://www .ncbi.nlm.nih.gov/pubmed/20938727). Therefore, it's so important to start healthy financial socialization at home, at a young age.

Consider the science of habits. Researcher Wendy Wood in her work ("Habits: A Repeat Performance," August 2006) found that 40 to 45% of the decisions we make every day aren't actually decisions, they are habits. Think about the implication of this as adults. We are walking around every day and 40% of what we actually do is based on something we may have learned decades ago, something that may or may not be positive, simply a learned behavior, most likely from our parents or major influencers from our formative years. Almost half of what we are doing every day is habit. For us as adults it requires some rewiring in order to change these habits, so the first step is to understand how these habits are formed, being mindful that they exist, and learn how to create new ones.

Within neurology the habit loop helps to explain how habits are created and how they function. The image shown here is from Charles Duhigg's book, *The Power of Habits* (Random House, 2012). This is a framework for either creating or changing a habit. The framework consists of four parts: have a plan, create a routine, provide rewards, and isolate the cue. The plan is the reason for the habit, the routine is the action you take, the reward is the items that positively reinforce the habit, and the cue is the trigger that initiates our routine.

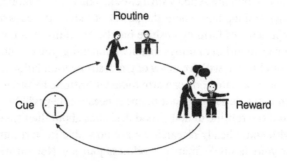

Much of what we do with our finances is mindless, so bringing mindfulness into our financial lives starts with being mindful of our good and bad habits and course correcting when necessary. The nice thing about our children is that they are, as they say in psychology, *tabula rasa*, or a blank slate. We as parents and influencers have the power, through financial socialization, to provide them with good habits to carry them through the rest of their lives. Let's dissect financial socialization as an example in practice. The basic foundation of financial wellness is to have control over one's finances. In order to have control one must have a plan for the monies that are earned; here for the positive financial socialization we will have a planned purpose for the money that comes into our accounts each month. For negative or neutral financial socialization, we will not have a plan.

	Positive Financial Socialization	Negative Financial Socialization
Routine	When I receive a paycheck I save 25% of my earnings	When I receive a paycheck it goes into my checking account
Cue	Receiving the paycheck triggers my mindful savings and action	Money in my account
Reward	Small: Each month seeing increase in savings and feeling in control Big: Retire early/buy the new house/fund education, etc.	Spend it all
Result	Clarity of purpose and realization of planned reward	Spending without thought and purpose; no savings to accomplish your goals, no clarity or control of financial resources

In the above example, savings 25% of earned income is a big deal and certainly requires willpower, particularly for adults who are trying to change habits. But for children, they won't know any different. You can teach willpower by deciding a reaction ahead of time. Teaching ahead of time will give your children the tools and action plan when presented with a circumstance. I earn money; I save money. When Charles Duhigg talks about the power of habits, the cues and rewards are critical components of forming positive habits. As adults, if you engage in mindfulness and pay attention to things that are happening, you can change any habit. Preparing our children with a catalog of good, strong foundational habits through positive financial socialization can arm them with strong habits, eliminating their need to even make decisions about finances because they will be hardwired with willpower and the routine to make good decisions about their finances.

Armed with some heady research we are now able to start putting the pieces together for your family's financial wellness journey. Not surprisingly, though, many families avoid the topic of money like the plague. Many parents simply think they don't have the tools to pass on savvy financial skills to their children. In truth, it is not that complicated, but like every other skill it takes time and attention. This is a commitment, but one that will pay dividends in more ways than one. Consider that when children are 18, in the eyes of the law, we have crowned them *adults*. They can execute a contract to take out a loan for a car, buy a house, and execute a student loan contract. Most 18-year-olds I know are ill-prepared for all of the above. As parents, we can no longer afford to be completely unconscious of our spending and savings patterns. Find teachable moments that interest your children, simplify the abstract of paying online or using a credit card with an explanation of how things work, and take every opportunity to give your children hands-on experience in saving, spending, sharing, and investing.

Money-Minded Motivation

- ✔ Financial socialization is a learned process of acquiring knowledge and developing skills. Use this book to acquire the knowledge to develop new skills for yourself and your family.
- ✔ Financial wellbeing can be learned and practiced like any other life skill.
- ✔ Conscious spending and saving will not only help you meet your financial goals, it will demonstrate the same skills for your children.
- ✔ Find teachable moments about your child's favorite store to talk about budgeting to buy their favorite things.
- ✔ Explain to your child how a credit card works and why you are using it.
- ✔ When possible, have your child pay or participate in a spending decision.
- ✔ Habits are the strongest foundation for healthy financial wellness.

4

Our Money Personalities

Before we can teach our children about money matters, we must first understand and become aware of our own relationship with money and how it shapes our own financial wellness. I grew up in a blue-collar community with a father who worked in banking. After serving in Vietnam, my father got a job at Girard Bank in Philadelphia. He met my mother while working there and hoped to keep working forever.

Though he had a steady white-collar job, we were lower middle class from a socioeconomic standpoint and always struggled with the bills. He left at 7:00 a.m. and was home at 4:30 p.m. every day. He did not have a profession, but rather a job. My mom worked odd jobs and neither of my parents had a college degree. Both were extremely intelligent; they just never had the support financially or otherwise to attend college.

Talking about money in our house was taboo. My parents considered it disrespectful to ask the kinds of curious questions that kids always have: How much does Dad make? How much is our house worth? Do we have a bank account? A savings account?

I remember hearing about a friend's dad who made $100,000 a year. At age 15, $100,000 sounded like a fortune to me. When I asked my mom how much my dad made, I was told it was none of my business and how *dare* I ask such a question. I felt ashamed and embarrassed. After that, I always felt a sense of misfortune for our family. My parents quarreled regularly about finances. Money became associated with negative emotion.

Although money was a dark subject for us, it made me curious and I wanted to understand more. My curiosity led me to want more. My parents didn't have money to buy me the latest and greatest clothes or "stuff." They simply said no. I thought they didn't think I was a good kid and took their "no" as an indication that I wasn't enough. My self-esteem fell so low that I ended up shoplifting in order to get the latest pair of Guess jeans and Champion sweatshirts in order to feel better about myself. Never once did my parents ask where my clothes came from—that is, until I got caught.

I think I'm a pretty extreme case of what happens when parents don't discuss money with children, but I share this because I wonder, what if instead of shaming me for asking questions, they told me, "Honey, we have enough to provide you, your brother, and your sister with food and housing, but we are on a very limited budget so many of the things you want, we can't afford. We work hard for what we have and someday you will work hard and, hopefully, you'll be able to afford the things you want."

There were ways to make the money conversation approachable and honest, without revealing my dad's salary or the cost of the house. Even without actual figures, I could have developed an understanding that our money was limited, and that it *wasn't* because I was inadequate as a daughter or person.

My husband grew up in the polar-opposite environment. His family members knew the cost of everything. They worked hard but also never wanted for anything. Money wasn't a taboo subject. In fact, money was consistently discussed, carefully spent, and always accessible. There was no shame in talking about money.

When my son was born in 2006, we spent a lot of time discussing the seemingly endless aspects of raising him: discipline, religion, education, extracurricular activities, daycare, and so on. Never once, however, did we discuss our "money personality" or how we would communicate our values regarding money with our son. I assume this is true for most of you reading this book as well. We both had several successful working years behind us and as a result had our own checking/savings and brokerage accounts. We only combined resources in order to pay our "joint" expenses, which were mostly the cost of our home.

Reflecting on my own experience, it is no wonder many parents find themselves in a situation where it seems like everything *but* finances is discussed when raising a child. College aside, how many parents have the discussion about what the cost of a child (or two or three) will do to their ability to save and their need to spend? Not many. Fortunately, like everything else, we somehow manage through it. But I submit to you that simply getting through it isn't good enough anymore. We need to raise our kids to be financially well; we have no choice but to develop our money-minded families with purpose.

I still remember when my son was four and we moved from Pennsylvania to South Carolina. My son asked how much our house cost. I was prepared to have an elaborate discussion in which I did not disclose the price but rather how the cost of things doesn't matter, when my husband quickly responded, "$642,000." I almost fell off my chair. My son didn't, nor should he, feel bad about asking, and my husband and I were careful to help him understand that we worked hard to get what we had and that moving to South Carolina was a goal of ours and through hard work and planning we were able to reach our goals. The conversation was open and positive, and I'm glad that even at such a young age, we began to foster a positive relationship with money for him that will hopefully serve him well throughout his formative years and into adulthood.

Despite the open, honest conversation, I still find myself cringing when discussions about how much we make or how much something costs come up with Jacob. It still feels unnatural to me, so I always add the caveat that salaries are personal. It's up to Daddy and me to share if we feel it appropriate, okay? A dose of humility, and no bragging. Jacob is what I call "money curious." He is always curious about the cost of items, and loves flashy cars and a stroll through a Gucci store. Though I do like that he isn't intimidated by money, it is a very different upbringing than I had. As a child, I would probably never have walked into a Gucci store because I would have been intimidated. He isn't a big spender, but definitely likes the finer things. I believe this is also part of the world we live in. When I was raised there were fewer means to access luxury items; today they are constantly splashed about in our daily newsfeeds. This is part of our history and impacts the money personality of our family.

Our family has a clearly defined, conscious "money personality" and even a family mission statement (which I discuss at the end of this book) to help us socialize our son according to our beliefs and goals while recognizing and appreciating our personal hang-ups. I believe that when we understand our money personalities and how our environment impacts our thoughts and actions, then we can create the opportunity to control our spending, saving, sharing, and investing instead of letting money control us. Understanding our money personalities helps us gain perspective over our habits; the better we understand why we are doing something, the easier it is to change. This is how we can start to create good habits and eliminate the bad ones.

How did you develop your money personality? What did you experience watching your own parents' and caretakers' habits with money? It's important to revisit your experiences as a child to develop an understanding of how your habits—good or bad—developed, and then to consciously decide how to communicate with your children so they (and you) will develop good habits and ultimately a healthy relationship with money. Remember we discussed the habit loop? Think about how simple we can make our children's lives if we give them the tools to put good financial habits into practice as soon as they are present with the cues. How will they learn this? Through financial socialization, which is foundationally communicating and emulating sound financial practices. Understanding your money personality and that of the other adults who influence your children can help you develop the communication methods that work best for your family.

While there is no shortage of additional "personality quizzes," books, and articles about different money personalities—in particular as they relate to differences between spouses—most research regarding financial behavior splits money personalities into only two categories: those with self-control or willpower and those without. Those that lack self-control are considered compulsive spenders and bad planners while those with self-control tend to be able to control their spending urges and have healthy long-term planning habits. Yet, just as we can't categorize our overall personalities as simply good or bad, we can't categorize our money personalities into two simple categories. There are simply too many layers and pounds of baggage.

I came across some research that endeavored to fine-tune the definition of money personalities, expanding beyond those with self-control versus no self-control. In an article in the *Journal of Behavioral and Experimental Finance* (May 2017), C. Stomback et al. attempt to differentiate money personalities by exploring both objective and subjective feelings about money, which lead to a wide range of financial behaviors.

The study found that, in addition to having self-control, optimism and deliberate thinking impact positive financial behaviors and lead to decreased anxiety about financial matters. It also found that today, financial behaviors tend to be more complex and extreme compared to those of previous generations. This is not surprising, due to the endless purchasing options and easy access we have to spending options in the digital world. The study reiterates that there is generally very little time or distance between us and our next purchase, and this creates new challenges few of us are adept in handling, specifically as it continues to challenge our self-control.

Beyond the academic research, there are some additional sets of money personalities that many of us can relate to. Instead of the limiting categorizations of putting people in groups of those with self-control versus those lacking self-control, I prefer the expanded set of money personalities as outlined by *The Financial Times*. They have identified six financial personality types—they even have their own quiz if you need a bit more guidance (https://ig.ft.com/sites/quiz/psychology-of-money/).

Anxious Investor: Action biased, overconfident, loves risk, and may have addictive personality

Hoarder: Risk-averse; money represents security

Social Value Spender: Loves to shop; may use money as a proxy for love and affection; tends to overspend

Cash Splasher: Uses money to be admired; may be very flashy; loves social media

Fitbit Financier: Extremely controlling, constantly evaluating; regularly switches service providers to find the best deal; do-it-yourselfers

Ostrich: Seldom opens financial statements; lacks long-term decision-making skills; generally believes that ignorance is bliss

Which do you most relate to?

Bernie and I have two very different money personalities, according to *The Financial Times* quiz. I am a Social Value Spender and Bernie is a Hoarder—these are two extremely different personalities. However, no one fits squarely into one personality type. Let me explain the Social Value Spender in me.

I *love* gift giving and I am keenly aware that I "stress-shop" to make myself feel better. In fact, I recently shared a story while speaking at a conference about my self-sabotage patterns that include stress-shopping. Sometimes my stress shopping goes so far that while I'm at Whole Foods shopping for our weekly meals, I find myself swinging by the clothing section to grab a scarf or perhaps a shirt. Yes, Whole Foods has a clothing section. When I look down at my shopping cart and see a sweater next to the Brussels sprouts and almond milk, I know I am stressed! These little purchases often give me a momentary high and satisfy me and may even preclude me from shopping online or heading to the pricier shops where some more severe spending damage may take place. I am aware of my "triggers" and have found little ways to appease my money personality's desires. One of the other traits of my money personality, at its extremes, is spending so much that I go into debt. Fortunately, I have curbed this aspect of my money personality and do not spend enough to result in debt. I recognize that some of my purchases may be deemed frivolous, but they make me happy and I don't allow them to damage my financial wellbeing. Understanding and managing your money personality is the key to financial wellbeing. Like anything, it is the extremes that are dangerous.

At the other end of the spectrum is Bernie, aka the Hoarder. For Hoarders, money represents security. Hoarders tend to be risk averse. Perhaps some hoarders even hide their money under the proverbial mattress. Bernie is not an extreme case, but he is very cautious and careful with our money. He has been known to clip coupons and, given the chance, will take a free sample or two. He is a sucker for a BOGO (buy one get one) special. At times, he can be what I would consider frugal, and other times he is not frugal at all. What's ironic is that you'd think our personalities would be the opposite of what they are, given the households in which we were raised. In mine, money was very tight, yet I now tend to stress-spend; in Bernie's, money was readily available, yet he now tends to hoard. Once again, this reinforces the point that the actual amount of a family's wealth has no bearing on money personality. Instead, it is the financial socialization experienced within the family that leads to our money personalities.

I am sure this makes your wonder how in the world we can guide our son Jacob (or you!) together with any sense of clarity. The first step is to simply be aware of and own your money personality. What does money mean to you? Security? Freedom? Opportunity? Fear? Anxiety? Power? Consider your thought process, or lack thereof, when it comes to how you decide to make or not make a purchase. Determine how you relate to money and then evaluate how you spend it and the relationship between the two.

We are all human, so we are perfectly imperfect. We have triggers, or things that set us off and cause reactions. Often, we may have negative reactions to certain triggers, like overspending or over-saving in response to anxiety about things beyond our control. Whatever your trigger, learn to recognize it and manage it.

For me personally, as I mentioned, my overspending can be caused by stress, lack of control, or wanting to please others. Bernie's hoarding tendencies are triggered by stress and fear. Recognizing these behaviors allows us to have conversations about our spending with Jacob. We often will use Bernie's hoarding tendencies, many of which are positive, to teach Jacob, for example, why we shop for the best deal, why we turn the lights off when we leave the room, how using coupons can save hundreds of dollars, and why saving and paying ourselves first and saving for all of our collective future is more important than any of our "things." We use my social value spending as an example of why spending money on others is important to us, and how giving gifts is not about the size or price of the gift, but about showing others that you care and are thinking of them. We teach him how important it is to be charitable with our time, talents, and treasures and why spending money on travel aligns with our family values. On the flipside, we also teach him about the lots of mistakes or "teachable moments" we have. We try to show him how sometimes we buy things we don't need and why that's okay when deliberate and thoughtful (sometimes) decisions are made, as long as the financial impact is not detrimental to our goals.

A prime example of our different money personalities in action and using them to help Jacob learn about finances took place on one of our annual ski vacations. Bernie, ever the hoarder, was seduced by a Vacation Club sales call. "Come spend an hour and a half of your time with us and we will give you your last night of vacation for free." Bernie was sold on the word "free," and in his defense, the offer was a $600 savings that sounded enticing. So, we spent two hours in the sales office listening to all the additional free items we would receive if we signed up for the Vacation Club program. We were hook, line, and sinker for the sale—but for different reasons. Bernie was interested in the savings we would get using "points" for multiple vacations throughout each year, while I was intrigued by the one super-high-end vacation we could take that would amp up our annual ski trip. Of course, we had to decide immediately, or the "deals" would expire. We provided our information and said we would come back the next day to sign all the paperwork.

Fortunately, we had a few moments of clarity when we put some distance between the deal and ourselves. That night, we had a long, deliberate discussion, with Jacob present, about the financial impact of committing to such an arrangement. Would we truly save money? Did the potential savings outweigh our need for flexible travel to different locations and properties? Could we find other ways to save money on travel without being as restrictive as this deal would require? Was the idea of staying at the super-high-end resorts as important as finding great locations that provided activities that offered quality time for our family to be together?

This is a great example of how we were able to put time between ourselves and our purchase, exhibit self-control, and use deliberate thinking to make an informed decision about a purchase while including Jacob in the discussion to further our efforts to financially socialize him. We ultimately opted for the purchase and both feel good about the decision.

This type of analysis can be done with any purchase you make, whether big or small. Including your children in your thought process, whether buying a car or buying a toaster, you are faced with so many choices; taking the time to thoughtfully work through your decisions and sharing them with your children will begin to teach them these same invaluable skills.

As we have discussed, our money personalities are formed largely by the influence of our parents and caretakers. But we can't discount how *when* we were born shapes our money personalities as well. Each generation has redefined the "American Dream" according to its own experiences. Our financial belief systems reflect both our upbringing as well as the external events surrounding us during our formative years. All these experiences influence how we view money and wealth as well as our ability to achieve that American Dream.

For example, if you are lucky enough to have known anyone who lived through the Great Depression, you likely know that what they experienced scared them and impacted their behavior for the rest of their lives. I remember my grandmother never throwing out a container. She not only reused every mayonnaise and milk jar, but scraped mold off cheese, mended her clothes, and fixed her furniture rather than replacing anything. In her generation, credit was something used only for a mortgage. She lived until 90 and never changed her ways. Contrast this with the behavior of those who came of age in the 1980s, when excess became the expectation and, consequently, consumer debt exploded. Today, those born into Generation Z, like my son, see exponential growth in virtually everything around them. Everything they need, want, and desire is readily available, as is access to debt. For this generation, controlling behavior and impulses in an era when we can have anything almost instantaneously is becoming more and more critical to creating and maintaining financial wellbeing.

When we were born plays a large role in shaping our money personalities. In fact, many believe that generations who are generally characterized by prudence and sacrifice tend to be followed by generations focused on leisure and feelings, rather than hard work and sacrifice. Thorstein Bunde Veblen was an American economist and sociologist who became famous as a witty critic of capitalism. Veblen identified something called *conspicuous consumption*, a characteristic of generations that consume without manufacturing. "In general terms, they lack a spirit of sacrifice because they abhor the notion of objective values and so lack the will to re-create or advance the social ethos created by their parents' generation" (*The Theory of the Leisure Class*, 1899). We see this in the generation that followed the "Greatest Generation." The *Boomers* fit the classic definition of a *leisure class*.

Consider experiences that have shaped money personalities over the generations:

1901–24: The Greatest Generation
People were living longer than previous generations, and new words like "senior citizen" entered the lexicon to accommodate the changes. Affluent society and "retirement" were introduced. People of this generation tended to want a steady job and a simple future, and house big enough for only husband and wife.

1925–40: The Silent Generation
When the Silent Generation was coming of age, the economy was booming, jobs provided great wages, and pensions were easy to find. They tended to marry young. "Eighty percent of life is just showing up" rings true for this era. They were the healthiest, wealthiest, and most educated.

1940–60: The Boomers
The most populous generation to date, Boomers are categorized as being careless about wealth, sometimes called "the leisure class." As Veblen details, "Boomers mark the apogee, and then the decline in generational progress as measured by real dollar income." Their focus was on individualism, risk-taking, and inner search. Out of necessity, they have had to retire later with less money and declining benefits as they are the first to experience the decline in "safe" retirement. Today, more than one-third of our federal budget pays benefits to those 65 and over, mainly to the Boomers.

1961–81: Generation X
The most unequal generation in terms of wealth, Gen X (which I am smack-dab in the middle of) grew up with hands-off parents, failing schools, and a skyrocketing divorce rate. Gen Xers' goal is to be well-off financially. Many started earning and investing when markets were at their highest valuations in the 1990s and were the hardest hit by the crash of the 2000s. This generation shows the biggest decline in homeownership.

1982–2004: The Millennials

Millennials watched their parents experience economic recession, and this fear dominates their view of the economy. Millennials have high standards for higher education, as their difficulty in finding secure, salaried careers has often resulted in their putting their lives on hold. They tend to marry, have kids, and purchase homes later. Their parenting style is to be very involved. Burdened by college loan debt and their risk-averse natures, they have taken a big jump to the lower middle class. Despite the bad rap they are often given, this is an optimistic and achievement-oriented generation.

Born after 2005: Generation Z

This generation is already estimated to have a collective spending power of $44 billion. The highly influential Gen Zers are the first digital-native generation. Most parents of Generation Z kids entered our teenage years without an email account and left for college without a cell phone. Facebook didn't exist and neither did the Internet. Gen Z parents tend to be "helicopter parents," mostly because we have no earthly idea how to raise children in this era of new social pressures. We worry that our kids are entitled, as I am sure all generations of parents have. Today, virtually everything is available immediately, and parents are finding that it's hard to teach this generation that all good things are worth waiting for when, let's be honest, there is rarely a wait for anything.

Certainly, these are generalizations and we each have our own unique experiences that shape our individual money personalities. The point is that each generation is influenced by different forces—political, economic, and social. The world we are born into helps shape our opportunities, experiences, and our views about money as much as the households we grew up in.

With the history lesson behind us, let us agree that it is foolhardy to alter our current reality back into history. That is, assume that things will continue as they did for our parents' and grandparents' generations. We certainly need to be clear on where we are and how we got here. We can and should learn the lessons from the past, but we must also be mindful that our current environment is quite different, and our current reality demands new thinking and new strategies, from us, for our children.

Now that you have a better understanding of our collective history around personal finance, the challenges we face, and I hope, a shared belief that our children must start early and often, building a strong foundation of financial literacy with parents, grandparents, and family members leading the way, let's get to work. With most things in life, the actual practice of the "thing," whether a job, a sport, or a performance, is the culmination of our dedication, of our suffering, if you will. Greatness and wellbeing take time, but it takes more than just time. Time alone simply ages us, but time spent with a meaningful focus on where we want to go in our lives takes hard work and determination and a perspective shift. I firmly believe, based on the issues facing us and our children today, we must all shift our perspective from what we knew to what we need to know in order to survive and thrive in the new world in which we find ourselves. Change the window through which you view the world and the world will become more accessible.

It was Maya Angelou who said, "When you know better, you do better." I like to say that not only when you know better, but when you know and define "your why," you not only do better, you succeed. It is not quite as elegant as Maya, but I think just as profound. There is a section in this book that will introduce you to the principles of money management. These tools are basic modules to help you learn the lessons of personal finance—investing, saving, spending, sharing—and should be among the tools to help you and your children become financially well. Implementing these tools should lead your family to increased savings, smarter investing, and generally a healthier balance sheet. All of these things may lead to a large bank account or 401(k) account, but alone will not keep you on the path to financial wellness if your mindset isn't right. So, before we jump into the principles of money management, let's focus on our mindset.

Money-Minded Motivation

- ✔ Take the money personality quiz to understand your starting point https://ig.ft.com/sites/quiz/psychology-of-money/).
- ✔ Evaluate your decisions in light of your newfound personality.
- ✔ Embrace your family's money personalities and understand the positive and negative lessons you can learn from them.
- ✔ Money is a leading cause of stress, but try to use deliberate thinking in order to increase positive financial behaviors and decrease anxiety about financial matters.
- ✔ Understand how your generation has influenced your money mindset and how your child's generation is influencing theirs.

5

Gaining a Healthy Perspective on Money

Let's begin with the simple word *money*. We all need it, we all have it, some more than others, but what does it represent to us? What comes to your mind when you hear the word *money*?

I did my own little experiment through a simple Facebook survey and received lots and lots of responses. Some of the favorites where quite humorous!

Money as a term of endearment: Does anyone remember Vince Vaughn in the movie *Swingers* saying, "You are sooooo *money* and you don't even know it"?

Money in musical lyrics: Pink Floyd, Abba, Cardi B, and The O'Jays. Can you hear the songs in your head?

The lyrics below span a few different generations, but the context is the same. We need money; we never have enough money; the love and desire for money can tempt one to do bad things. I couldn't include Cardi B's lyrics here (this is a family book), but trust me when I say her sentiments are very similar.

Money

Pink Floyd

Money, get away
Get a good job with good pay and you're okay
Money, it's a gas
Grab that cash with both hands and make a stash
New car, caviar, four-star daydream
Think I'll buy me a football team

Money, Money, Money

ABBA

Money, money, money
Must be funny
In the rich man's world

Money, money, money
Always sunny
In the rich man's world
Aha, aha
All the things I could do
If I had a little money
It's a rich man's world
It's a rich man's world

For the Love of Money

The O'Jays .

Money-money-money-money-money [Repeat: x 6]
Some people got to have it
Some people really need it
Listen to me why'all, do things, do things, do bad things with it
You want to do things, do things, do things, good things with it
Talk about cash money, money
Talk about cash money-dollar bills, why'all
For the love of money
People will steal from their mother
For the love of money
People will rob their own brother
For the love of money
People can't even walk the street
Because they never know who in the world they're gonna beat
For that lean, mean, mean green
Almighty dollar, money
For the love of money
People will lie, Lord, they will cheat
For the love of money
People don't care who they hurt or beat

In a YouTube video, Julie Andrews, of *Mary Poppins* fame, explains to Stephen Colbert how to smile for a picture. She says to have the photographer count to 3 and instead of saying the standard "cheese" say "money." She goes on to explain that it forces a smile on anyone's face. (It works! I've tried it ever since seeing the interview.)

That isn't to say that money always elicits a happy response. Some of the responses I also received were fear, greed, don't have enough, worry, anxiety—the root of all evil. Others saw money as a means to an end, college, braces, retirement, vacations, shopping spree, and so on. Clearly money is a trigger for all, whether it is humor, fear, or opportunity.

In her book, *The Soul of Money* (W. W. Norton, 2003), Lynn Twist helps us focus on what is truly important. She points out that we tend to give the word *money* so much power that it can cripple and control us. We need to gain a different perspective on the meaning of money and recognize that *money doesn't define who we are. Rather richness comes from the soul, spirit, character, and values.*

In the book, Lynn helps us explore how the unconscious, unexamined mindset spends without thought while an informed mindset aligns values with resources and is rewarded for having self-discipline. So, in order to take away the crippling power of money, we must shift our focus from spending to earning, and let the driver of our personal economies move from self-interest to self-knowledge. What a wonderful lesson to pass to your children. *Money is just a thing; never make the mistake of giving it your power.* Use money as a tool to enhance your personal economy. Your *personal economy* can be defined as the things in life that truly matter: your family, your home, your passions, and your career. Everyone has one. Yours is as unique to you as your fingerprint and is constantly evolving.

In another wonderful book, *Your Money or Your Life* (Penguin, 1993), Joe Dominguez gives us another way to view money. He says, "The only thing you can say that is always true for you, 100% of the time: Money is something you trade your life energy for." Life energy? The first time I read that line, I stopped dead in my tracks. How amazingly profound! The book goes on to explain that once you firmly believe that you are trading your life energy—your time, your talents, the hours of your life, your personal economy—for money, then you begin to view the way you earn and spend money through a different lens. It's all a trade-off.

Consider a teenager with her first job, making $150 for a full week working in a retail store or a sandwich shop. She'd prefer to be at the pool with her friends, or really anywhere else. On her day off, she goes shopping. She sees a pair of jeans that are the newest craze, pulls the tag and reveals a price of $150. She stops, thinks before spending: *Is a full week of my time worth trading for a new pair of jeans?* Today, there are fewer malls to shop in, and she most likely saw the newest trends on Instagram and clicked through to see the price. Either way, the perspective is the same. There is no right or wrong answer; spending money is personal but being mindful and informed about what we are willing to trade our time and our life energy for can help us begin to truly understand and define what we value. This exercise will serve us and our children well in all aspects of their life.

Identifying what we value and determining how we want to spend our life energy forces us to make conscious financial choices in our lives. As history has shown us, we have more available to us than we could ever need or consume. The abundance of things we have access to has liberated us but hasn't fulfilled most of us. Our children will continue to be faced with chasing more and more stuff; in fact having access to so much has even changed the way in which we desire things. We want more because we can have more. Grounding our children with values and goals can help our children manage the abundance they will face.

Like everything else in life, financial wellbeing requires having some balance. I'm not advocating teaching children extreme frugality, but rather that we understand our financial values and develop positive financial habits to support those values. We need to define and help our children develop their own baseline. People I work with who align their values with spending generally spend less. Like our political preferences, most will fall somewhere in between frugality and extravagance. Teaching our children to plan a financial life that supports their goals and dreams is an important part of financial socialization. After all, as Gloria Steinem said, "Without leaps of imagination or dreaming, we lose the excitement of possibilities. Dreaming after all is a form of planning."

So, how and when do we begin? Just like when to start saving and when to teach your child about values and goals it should be early and often. Starting a healthy financial socialization process with your children at a young age is important to helping them develop financial wellbeing later in life. While you may think a preschooler should be focused on learning colors, shapes, and how to share her toys, this is also the perfect time to begin introducing financial concepts. Of course, you must personalize and tailor your lessons to your child's age and ability to conceptualize. But a preschooler's love of imaginative play can lend itself well to the basic tenets of finance.

These same concepts can be taught early on until they are incorporated into your child's daily life. We are faced with financial decisions multiple times a day, far more than we are faced with a geometry problem or having to write a haiku, so let's start now making sure our children are armed with the knowledge they need to succeed in today's world.

It is never too early to let kids engage in play that helps them build a healthy relationship with money and begin to understand financial concepts. Preschool years are when children begin to see the world around them. The National Association of Early Childhood Education advocates for what they call "playful learning" at this age, a combination of free play and guided play.

Research studies have shown that the relationship between children's play and development in several areas—including language and executive function—is a critical component to understanding financial concepts and creating meaningful goals. In fact, findings show that imaginative play is such a valuable method of teaching that it fosters the precise context that facilitates learning.

One such study, "The Science of Learning," identified four key ingredients of successful learning. The study showed that learning occurs best when children are mutually active (not passive), engaged (not distracted), socially interactive (as adults), and building meaningful connections (*Source:* Linda Darling-Hammond,

Lisa Flook, Channa Cook-Harvey, Brigid Barron, and David Osher (2019), "Implications for Educational Practice of the Science of Learning and Development," *Applied Developmental Science*, DOI: 10.1080/10888691.2018.1537791).

The red cash register my son had when he was a preschooler was a great example of how imaginative play can develop an exchange of knowledge and skills as it relates to financial wellness. It came with a drawer full of paper money, coins, and a credit card. Attached to it was a type of conveyor belt and a scale to weigh items. He would spend hours pushing buttons, swiping cards, taking money, giving change (sometimes giving back way more than what was paid!). He would weigh plastic fruit, shoes—anything and everything. I remember there were times I felt I had to teach him by explaining things like using a credit card and making correct change. Not only was he too young to understand the concepts, he just didn't care. He was having a blast simply playing. What he was learning, however, were the basic concepts of economics. He was learning that there is a cost for goods and a process by which we buy and sell them. As he got a little older, he began to understand the values of goods and services as well as supply and demand. When there was only one red apple left, I would often be charged $100.

Finding ways to create an environment where your children are active, engaged, social, and building meaningful connections between their play and their knowledge is extraordinarily powerful and fun. There are so many tools to help young children roleplay, including children's museums with kid-sized grocery stores and takeout restaurants. I love watching kids play there.

I once worked with a great salesperson who would say, "Tell them what you're going to say, say it, and then tell them what you have said." While this may be from Sales 101, it applies so much to parenting as well. We can use "play learning" to create the foundation for financial literacy and to reinforce basic concepts by saying it, showing it, repeating it, and then doing it all over again. In this manner, elementary school children can begin with relative ease to understand deeper concepts of personal finance and understand the consequences of actions and carry these lessons into the real world as they get older.

The last few chapters have focused on *you*—where your habits came from and your personal money history, personality, and mindset. This was intended to create in you a deep curiosity, evaluation, and foundation for moving forward—for yourself and your family—on your financial wellness journey. With the introspective behind you, I encourage you now to put the building blocks together in order to have money work for you. Like any business, if you are clear with your strategy and your goals and objectives, your employees will be clear about their purposes and their objectives. Think of money as the tool, or the employee, that is working for you. With clarity of purpose and vision, it will help you achieve your dreams and open up opportunities to fulfill your and your family's personal wealth journey.

Next we will focus on how you can help your children become financially literate. We haven't talked much about financial literacy, which tends to be a bit of a buzzword these days. *Financial literacy* is the set of skills and knowledge of financial matters that allow a person to make informed decisions about their finances. Most of the advocacy and promotion for financial literacy focuses on adults, and specifically on improving statistics about our nation's savings rate (or rather lack thereof) toward retirement. I find many of these approaches are a little too late. It's almost never too early to introduce financial literacy concepts to our children, no matter their age. There have been a growing number of schools across the country as well as nonprofits doing amazing work to get financial literacy programs into schools to help reinforce concepts that can be taught at home. This book will next focus on what I believe are the foundational elements of financial literacy and how to practice them, at every age, with your child. Please understand that alone, financial literacy may not lead to financial success. Knowing how to ride a bike and actually riding a bike are two very different things. This is why the first half of the book helps you develop mindfulness around finances so that what you learn can be applied in a way that leads you to financial wellness.

There are five major concepts that frame my foundation to build a strong personal financial wellness plan. I will discuss these categories in depth and provide examples for you to implement for yourself and your children, no matter what their age:

1) Baseline: Values and Goals
2) Freedom: Saving
3) Flow: Spending
4) Sharing
5) Investing

Money-Minded Motivation

- ✔ Money is just a thing; never make the mistake of giving it your power.
- ✔ Think in terms of your personal economy.
- ✔ Consider: What are you willing to trade your life energy for?
- ✔ Learning takes place best when people are active, engaged, social, and building meaningful connections. Create financial learning opportunities for your children that allow them to be active, not passive, participants in the process.

6

Your Baseline Values and Goals

In my financial planning practice, I work with people every day to help them achieve their goals. Most of my clients' goals involve things like helping save for children's college education, helping realize a dream of owning a business, retiring early, or creating a foundation that will live long after they are gone. All these things require people to really think about what is important to them, and what they value most. Once we determine what's important to us, we have our baseline and then we can build a plan to help accomplish those goals.

Values and goals serve to clarify, validate, and channel our behavior. While it can be difficult to define our goals, consider how one of my favorite financial thinkers, Carl Richards, in his book, *The One-Page Financial Plan* (2015), describes goals:

1) Goals are guesses. I'm giving you permission to relax as you think about goals. No one knows exactly what they are going to be doing 17.5 years from now. No sense in laboring over a false sense of precision. Guess. Just get started.
2) Goals are flexible. It's possible to be completely committed to a goal and at the same time open to changing it. Don't change your goal just because it turns out to be harder than you thought to reach it. But you can change it if it no longer represents what you think you want to do. Remember, it was a guess.
3) Goals are yours. Not your neighbor's or Instagram's. Yours.
4) Think big goals and micro-actions. Having a big, scary goal gets you out of bed. Repeatedly taking the next smallest step keeps you moving.

As difficult as it is for adults to create goals, for children we need to break the concept of goal setting down even further. People rarely reach goals they haven't set, so teaching kids how to make goals is another invaluable life lesson. Nearly every item children ask their parents to buy can become the object of a goal-setting discussion. And goal setting can help children learn to become responsible for themselves and help them reach for their personal dreams, not just financial ones.

When Jacob was in fifth grade, I was asked to come into his classroom to discuss setting goals and general planning concepts that could translate from financial planning to any area of life planning. The previous year, in fourth grade, the children had been introduced to the Stock Market Game, an online simulation of stock picking and research. It was interesting to me that schools teach our children to "pick stocks" before they even understand basic financial concepts, but that is another book. Nonetheless, in fifth grade, his teacher, Mrs. Bischoff, introduced the kids to the seven habits of highly effective people, which offers some amazing life skills, including "begin with the end in mind," which is central to goal setting. For my discussion, she wanted the focus to be on helping kids with their academic planning for the second half of the year. I came up with a plan to offer students guidelines on how best to set a goal for their grades and then build a personal plan to help make sure they achieved success.

When I told Jacob I was coming into his classroom to discuss goals, his first reaction was, "Like soccer goals? What do you know about soccer?" Next to nothing as it turns out, but this made me laugh and also validated my notion that young children aren't exposed to goal setting, but they *should* be. Most successful adults set goals for just about everything from running a marathon, to traveling to Senegal, to limiting our alcohol consumption to one (or three) nights a week. Goals are part of our daily lives and they help us become more successful at whatever it is we desire. Why not start our kids off to reach for success as early as possible?

As Jacob identified, a goal is like a target or something you shoot for. Soccer players shoot for goals and football players aim for touchdowns. But goals aren't just for sports. Some of the goals the children in Mrs. Bischoff's class wanted to achieve were:

- Learn to master a double pirouette.
- Become a better football quarterback.
- Get a scholarship to the Naval Academy for swimming.
- Spend less time on social media.

So, they clearly got the idea of *begin with the end in mind*, but when asked "why" or "how" they often fell short on answers. What they were missing is what I call the *why* power. To achieve something, we need to have a reason for wanting to achieve it. Seeking our *why* or our purpose is elemental to our human drive, often rooted in our values, and children just need to be guided.

When we set goals, we do it because there are things we want to achieve, obtain, or improve because it's important to us for some reason. We also need a plan to help us get there. The saying, "A goal without a plan is just a wish," reminds us that just saying, "I want to do xyzzy..." isn't enough. Many adults and kids today think and even dream in terms of instant gratification. I often remind Jacob that "you can have *anything*, but you can't have *everything*," because most things in life don't just come to us simply because we want them. We need to set goals, make plans, and have the drive to achieve them.

When helping kids to set goals, I think it's important to start in the nebulous world of dreams. Here, not everything makes its way to a goal, but we can be thoughtful and open to lots of ideas and vet them out.

I have culled a process for goal planning from several different financial and life management theories to create a process. This process can help children understand that their dreams can come true with focus, drive, and nurturing.

Eight Steps Toward Goal Planning with Purpose	
Dream	Articulate your dream.
Align values	Explore whether your dream aligns with your values and beliefs.
Visualize	Visualize what it feels like to achieve your dream. Without feeling passionate about your dream, it's not likely actionable.
Focus	Clearly define and focus on your goal using the SMART (is it Specific, Meaningful, Action-oriented, Realistic, Timely) process.
Define your Intention	How do you intend to reach your goal? Outline the steps necessary to achieve your goal. Create your to-do list.
Commit	Make a commitment to yourself that you will maintain the self-discipline needed to achieve your goal.
Inspire	Find inspiration each day to take the actionable steps to realize your goals. This will help you build confidence and also inspire others.
Investment	Identify your costs in terms of time, energy, and/or money.

Here are two examples in action:

Grace Hotchkiss, Age 16, Sophomore

Dream	To beat the high school state record for pole vault before I graduate.
Align values	Yes, because I believe it is important to reach my athletic and physical potential.
Visualize	I can visualize myself completing a vault of 13 feet, 1 inch.
Focus	Yes, it is all of those.
Define your Intention	I intend to go to practice three times a week for the next three years and work out to get stronger.

(Continued)

Commit	I have made a workout plan and have spoken to my coach about the things I must do.
Inspire	I find most of my inspiration from meeting others who share goals like mine and my teammates and coach.
Investment	None.

Grace has a laser focus on what she dreams about and has defined very specific and measurable steps to help her achieve her goals. Additionally, and critically, her dreams align with her personal values. The final step of "investment" is one we often overlook, as Grace did. Grace's investment is in time and energy. These things have real, tangible value. The time she spends practicing is time she is away from other activities. There are probably a few additional financial costs for her events and competitions, and perhaps a trainer. For Grace, these costs are most likely absorbed by her school or parents and may be unknown to her. Grace doesn't need to know the excruciating details of each expense, but perhaps knowing the value of her time and the financial investment her school and parents are making in her will help drive her even harder toward her goal. As I am writing my final draft, not only has Grace beat the HS State record in pole vaulting, she did so in her Sophomore year, is the #1 high school girl in SC, and was instrumental in her team winning the Girls' State title. She is now a Junior and all I can say is remember her name. She is a goal-setting, pole-vaulting queen!

Jacob Mackara, Age 12

Dream	Go to an elite college and play football.
Align values	I know that a good education is important to my family and it will help my future and playing sports is important to me for my personal growth.
Visualize	I can see myself at a really great school, meeting friends, getting great grades, and crushing it on the football field.
Focus	Yes, but maybe the school isn't specific enough yet.
Define your Intention	I will continue to work hard to obtain an A average and stay in all honors classes. I will also train to get stronger physically so that I can continue to compete at a very high level.
Commit	I have made a commitment to myself and my family that I will be the very best I can be.
Inspire	I find inspiration in many college athletes who commit to themselves, their schools, and their families.
Investment	College will be very expensive.

Jacob has a dream, one that will inevitably cause a significant investment of his time and talents, not to mention money to pay for school and all of the training that may be necessary. At age 12, these goals are long-term in nature. What I believe would be more effective is for him to break down what he wants to accomplish this year, his sixth-grade year of middle school. Then, further refine to identify what he will do to make straight A's and what he will do to train in order to perform at a high level. Each year, he can build a new plan that will align with his dream. As of my final edit, Jacob is now in seventh grade and is playing Junior Varsity football, has a five-day-a-week training schedule, and is making straight A's.

Smaller goals or purchases are pretty typical of elementary and middle-school children. Another of Jacob's goals was to buy a pair of the Apple Air pods. Though this really didn't align with his values (aside from being "cool" and "trendy") and his only true "inspiration" was the many athletes he sees wearing them pregame, he managed to use the latter part of this exercise to commit to specific savings goals in order to eventually purchase the Air pods.

For a simpler goal, like shorter-term purchases for kids and adults alike, I like the simplicity of WWH: Why? What? How?

Why is this important?
What will you do with it?
How are you going to obtain this item? How typically leads to a lesson on budgeting and money management.

I use this *every* time my son finds a new pair of sneakers he "has to have." Most often, after walking through WWH, he comes to his own decision that he doesn't want them anymore. Eventually, employing this practice can carry into all areas of life. It can help clarify personal values and establish spending plans to align with those values. It may even help inspire us to lead happier, more satisfying lives, because it empowers us to take control. Using *why* as the gatekeeper helps us pause and be much more mindful in our planning and purchasing.

The real work, of course, comes into play during the *how*, *focus*, and *intention* phases, when we get realistic about architecting and making tangible plans to achieve our goals. The to-dos should be rooted in small manageable chunks of time that align with meeting your children where they are. This process is a skill that will help your kids at school and later in their jobs. It's meant to set them up to succeed in anything they set out to accomplish.

There are a few issues we all face when dealing with goal setting. We are humans after all, and often find that our behaviors are not always aligned with our brains and we often act impulsively, particularly when it comes to buying things. As

Maya said, the more we know, the better we do, so here are just a few areas to consider and shift your perspective to help develop healthier habits for yourself and your family. Many of these are reinforced by the research that supports that notion that those who exercise self-control, deliberate thinking (planning), and optimism have better financial success. Introduce these concepts and words to your children by name, define them, and help them to master or at least begin to create awareness of each.

Instant Gratification. A critical component of healthy financial wellbeing is delaying instant gratification. No matter the wealth or lack of wealth passing from one generation to the next, a crucial finding in research shows that children who inherently have, or have learned, the skill of delayed gratification have better life outcomes, including financial health. The most famous and impressive research that I have found about instant gratification and self-control is the Marshmallow Experiment, performed by Stanford University professors Walter Mischel and Ebbe B. Ebbesen. In the experiment, preschool children were each given a marshmallow, and told they could eat it right away or that if they waited 15 minutes, they would get two marshmallows to eat. The majority, 67% of the children in the experiment ate the marshmallow right away, failing to resist temptation. The researchers followed all of the children for over five decades to determine how or if the ability to exercise self-control at an early age was correlated with various life outcomes as the children grew into adults. The results were truly impressive—children who resisted the simple marshmallow temptation were more successful in almost every outcome measured! They had higher SAT scores, were in better physical shape, and had higher educational attainment and other life measures. The seemingly simple ability to wait for what is to come, or learning the old adage, "Good things are worth waiting for," has a strong impact on future success. Many refer to this as self-control or willpower or having the grit to wait for what is to come.

Needs versus wants. Virtually every time we go to the store with our children, they ask for that new game, pair of jeans, iPhone cover, or a pack of baseball cards—anything within arm's reach of the checkout line. Instead of saying "yes" to appease them, or "no" to avoid resulting drama, simply ask, "Is that a need or a want?"

This simple question will cause your child to pause and consciously think about the purchase and frame it as a need or a want. You aren't yelling "I said *no*" or giving in at the last minute because they wore you down. Instead, you are giving them the tools to mindfully consider what they are asking you to buy and why. In my experience, the answer is "want" 9 times out of 10. Perhaps, after they admit it is a want, ask why and what. Why do you want it and what will you do with it? You may still choose to purchase the item for your child regardless of the answer; however, you will have planted a seed about the value of things, and this will begin to prepare your child for making smart spending decisions in the future. For older children who have money in their piggybank or savings account, this is a good time to introduce the concept of *how*, which includes budgeting (discussed in Chapter 7). How will *you* pay for it?

While I do not have scientific research outside of my experiences and observations with family and friends, I am confident in my belief that children who are given things after acting up, after parents have said no, have a difficult time developing financial impulse control. This lack of impulse control, which is apparent in many children and adults, has become a large problem in our society, as evidenced by the rampant, out-of-control credit card debt in our country. Instead of thoughtfully setting goals and planning for what we want, weighing risks and rewards, so many go straight for the reward, no questions asked. We rack up debt to accommodate those new shoes and gadgets we must have, and even buy houses we can't afford. Understanding the difference between needs and wants is crucial to controlling impulses and hopefully reducing our debt.

Advance purchase planning. It is important that children learn how to prioritize purchases in order to make wise choices. When you take your children to stores or shop online, instead of buying everything they want, explain how to plan purchases in advance and make price comparisons before pulling the trigger. For example, if you are looking for a new TV or home appliance, do your research and make your kids part of the process. Show them how much money they can save by doing research, and how holding off on those impulse purchases can result in the reward of having more money left over after the purchase.

For good or bad, our children have access to everything if they are on a phone/computer/tablet, so why not have them hunt for bargains and comparison shop for you? Have them develop an understanding of the financial impact of making unconscious purchases.

Consequences. Another critical lesson is that choices have consequences. As a general rule, unplanned spending, or making impulse purchases, results in 20 to 30% of our money being wasted. Yet, impulse buying is a common behavior trait. Our culture of consumption enables us to quickly succumb to temptation and make purchases before even considering the consequences. How many Amazon boxes do you see daily on porches in your neighborhood? How often have you ordered something off of impulse and actually forgot you ordered it until it showed up on your doorstep? Often, because we fail to do our research on our purchases or attach value to a "thing," we accumulate piles of things we neither need nor want any longer. Those piles can be lessons on smart-versus-careless spending choices.

You may say that is an awful lot to think about before buying a simple pack of gum. But I assure you these are invaluable concepts that will lead your children to a healthy financial life, and if repeated and reinforced over time will become second nature. Can children really learn these skills? Certainly they can. Creating an environment for our children where they experience small and large delays in gratification can help them foster more thoughtful interactions with their finances. The first thing to focus on is modeling self-discipline yourself. Be aware of your habits. Are you exhibiting self-control in your personal, financial, and emotional life? For your younger children, games like red-light-yellow-light-green-light-stop and follow the leader are a great way to reinforce self-control.

Another, no matter the age, is to make sure when at the checkout line you (or your children) don't become a victim to the point-of-purchase candy or nicely presented seasonal items placed beside the register. There is actual science behind the placement of these point-of-purchase items. In 1952, economist Hawkins Stern from Stanford Research Institute published a paper titled, "The Significance of Impulse Buying Today." Stern described a phenomenon he called *suggestion impulse buying*, which is "triggered when a shopper sees a product for the first time and visualizes a need for it." It's why we feel like we must have these items. Yet, it's important to teach children to resist the impulses to purchase these types of items, because truly, none of them are necessities. And it's the perfect time to have the needs-versus-wants discussion with your child (or with yourself).

Teaching impulse control is as simple as taking advantage of everyday teaching opportunities to reinforce some basic concepts. For example, consider all those impulse toy purchases that resulted in ownership of broken toys. This can be an opportunity to show your child customer feedback reviews that discuss the poor quality of an item, or to show them how comparing prices could have saved them money. All these types of lessons help reinforce advance planning. Planning and researching purchases puts space and time between willpower (or lack of it) and the purchase. The space and time allow you to initiate open discussion about spending pros and cons before more spending takes place. And do, please share your own stories. If you made a bad decision due to lack of research, impulse shopping, or something else, tell your children so that they can learn from your experiences. Use your experiences as examples to help them frame their choices, because eventually they will dive right in and choose, and all we can do is hope we have given them a strong jumping-off point.

None of this is intended to say that splurging is never okay. In fact, we all deserve a good splurge sometimes. But it's important to make sure we know they are splurges and that they are special, and not daily or weekly occurrences. After work, school, extracurricular activities, and our growing social obligations, it's important to also have fun while being mindful of the choices we make. In fact, this makes the splurges even sweeter.

The Smiths and the Jones. Have you heard the phrase, "shirt sleeves to shirt sleeves in three generations"? This is actually an English translation of the Lancashire proverb, "There's nobbut three generations atween a clog and clog." It means that wealth gained in one generation will be lost by the third. Various versions of this sentiment appear in many different cultures from Chinese to Irish to Italian to Spanish. The story goes that parents of the first generation, through grit and determination, clear the path for their children and grandchildren. They work incessantly to provide a life better than the one they grew up with. That grit is then lost on future generations as they begin to expect and rely solely on the first generation for support and do little to earn for themselves. This is the traditional thought behind the proverb. A new, healthier alternative to consider is that instead of creating expectations of wealth in our children we should create expectations of the same hard work and grit used to create the wealth. And that grit isn't something developed simply from having to struggle to overcome as the first generation did, but nurturing and growing the wealth that their parents and grandparents worked so hard for.

I personally have experience with two extreme examples of wealth transfer between generations and how expectations and communication through financial socialization in the family can deplete or increase wealth. The examples are of two families, each in their second generation with significant wealth—wealth created by the hard work and grit of their parents. Both families watched their parents work hard, earn and save money, and build wealth after starting with very little. I'll call the first family the Smiths. When I think of the Smiths, I am inspired by their grit and desire to work hard. They live below their means but meet their needs. They don't drive fancy cars or splash their money about. Instead, they spend on a few key categories that are in line with their belief systems. Within these categories, they give their intellectual, social, and financial capital generously. They see the financial successes of their parents as a gift to be cherished, cared for, respected, and valued—a gift they can add to and not detract from, and as a resource to grow, develop, and share with future generations. They align their resources with their family's values. This family has a mission statement to help guide them, along with regular meetings to discuss the family's resources.

Let's call the second family the Joneses. The Jones family views their parents' wealth and assets as a right—something that is due them. They spend without conscious thought. They squander the money left to and for them with little if any regard for the blood, sweat, and tears that generated it. I have often heard Jones family members say things like, "My mom left this money for me to do whatever I want." The Joneses have no family mission statement or central value system to help guide their future generations on how to spend their financial, social, and intellectual capital. As the saying goes, there most likely will not be a third generation of wealth for anyone to enjoy.

I often marvel at the differences between different families' behavior, and sometimes even between siblings within the same families. When I consider the differences between the Smiths and the Joneses, knowing these families personally provides a bit of insight. The Smith family, for example, was raised to expect little of others and a lot of themselves. In order to get what they have, they had to work for it—nothing was handed to them. "To whom much is given, from them much is expected," is a phrase that often comes to mind when I work with them. This is the epitome of the Smiths. Each family member was held accountable for emulating a clear set of defined values. They set clarity of purpose, intent, and expectation.

On the contrary, the Jones family's first generation worked extremely hard, but offered little structure when it came to financial discipline or expectations. The rules were loose; communication and guidance for how to spend was limited. And as a result, the second generation did not value or perpetuate their wealth.

It is important to take the lessons of these two families to your own family. The actual dollar amounts these families have doesn't matter; what matters is that the parents in both situations set the tone and the environment for their children's future behaviors. Our job is massive and overwhelming, but so very crucial to our children's future wellbeing.

Hunter S. Thompson on Finding Your Path

Not all children or adults have a clearly defined path. Many very smart and educated people truly struggle with life purpose and goal setting. For those people, I find words from Hunter S. Thompson inspirational.

In April 1958, Hunter S. Thompson was 22 years old when he wrote this letter to his friend, Hume Logan, in response to a request for life advice:

> We must make the goal conform to the individual, rather than make the individual conform to the goal. In every man, heredity and environment have combined to produce a creature of certain abilities and desires— including a deeply ingrained need to function in such a way that his life will be MEANINGFUL. A man has to BE something; he has to matter.

> As I see it then, the formula runs something like this: a man must choose a path which will let his ABILITIES function at maximum efficiency toward the gratification of his DESIRES. In doing this, he is fulfilling a need (giving himself identity by functioning in a set pattern toward a set goal), he avoids frustrating his potential (choosing a path which puts no limit on his self-development), and he avoids the terror of seeing his goal wilt or lose its charm as he draws closer to it (rather than bending himself to meet the demands of that which he seeks, he has bent his goal to conform to his own abilities and desires).

In short, he has not dedicated his life to reaching a predefined goal, but he has rather chosen a way of life he KNOWS he will enjoy. The goal is absolutely secondary: it is the functioning toward the goal which is important. And it seems almost ridiculous to say that a man MUST function in a pattern of his own choosing; for to let another man define your own goals is to give up one of the most meaningful aspects of life— the definitive act of will which makes a man an individual.

Let's assume that you think you have a choice of eight paths to follow (all predefined paths, of course). And let's assume that you can't see any real purpose in any of the eight. THEN— and here is the essence of all I've said— you MUST FIND A NINTH PATH.

Whether or not your children's path is already clear to them or they must create their own "ninth path," doing so will provide a level of clarity and purpose that will drive and inform their choices, especially their financial choices. We may change our path along the way, but if we don't define our path, we can feel constantly lost.

Money-Minded Motivation

- ✔ Just like when setting goals for life, setting goals for money requires you to be mindful and deliberate.
- ✔ Take the time to exercise Goal Planning with a Purpose. Walk through the process for both you and your child. Follow through and evaluate your and their success.
- ✔ Money is just a thing; never make the mistake of giving it your power.
- ✔ Remind your children: Abundance is within you, *not* in things.
- ✔ Teach your children to put time and space between their purchases and exercise Advanced Purchase Planning; this will help to eliminate the instant-gratification sickness we have.

7

Principles of Money Management: Save

As discussed earlier, I grew up with a father who was a banker and a mother who did not work outside our home. We never, *ever* spoke about finances. Because we never talked about it, I didn't think about money: how to spend it, save it, or value it. That all changed when I graduated from college burdened with both student loan and credit card debt. It took me years to undo these bad habits and get out of debt. As a result, I had no money to save. I started late and, fortunately, was able to move up in my career, and as I earned more money, I saved more money.

To this day, parents and even schools are woefully underprepared to teach our children about money management. Parents often lack the time and resources. Schools rarely make it part of their curriculum. This must change. In order to help our children develop invaluable financial skills as adults, we must embrace our role as teachers of money management by teaching them some basic concepts while they are young. My goal is to arm you with some basic tools to start this important dialogue. The foundation of managing money is saving. Knowing how to invest well and spend well is nothing if you can't save well. *Think of it not as saving but as purchasing freedom.*

The Richest Man in Babylon, by George S. Clason (Penguin, 1926), is one of the seminal books for teaching young men and women about personal finance. In the book, a man named Arkad, known as the richest man in Babylon, shares his success stories with those who were raised in very similar circumstances but, because of their poor financial decision making, ended up poor. The book illustrates the simple steps Arkad took to reach financial prosperity.

"Our prosperity as a nation depends upon the personal financial prosperity of each individual." This is the first sentence of *The Richest Man in Babylon*, first published in 1926. Yet it sounds like it was written today. Now is the time our children need to take back their future.

Clason's first and most important lesson is "Pay yourself first." This is perhaps the most important lesson your children can learn when they enter the working world or, better yet, when they get their first "gift of money." The concept supports the idea that part of what you earn should be yours to keep. What many people tend to do is to generate expenses that causes them to pay everyone but themselves and end up spending all of what they earn, or worse, *more* than what they earn. They pay the grocer, banker, clothing store, electric company, credit card company, and so on, but not themselves.

In order to pay ourselves first, we must spend less than we earn. Arkad suggests starting by saving 10% of what we earn as soon as we start earning. The sooner we begin this habit, the better off we'll end up financially. Paying ourselves first involves learning to live off the remainder of our paychecks by using a budget. Unless we "control thy expenditures," says Arkad, our "necessary expenses" will always grow to equal our incomes. This is true for so many people. The more we earn, the more things we think we need, the more money we have, and suddenly everything we have gets bigger: bigger houses, better cars, bigger vacations, and so forth. Do these bigger-and-better things align with our goals and values? So often we don't stop to ask these questions and our children are watching and learning.

The purpose of a budget is to "fatten thy purse" as told by Arkad. A budget should be reflective of desires and values and should serve as a defense against making purchases based on casual desires. Saving 10% versus spending that 10% on new shoes or technology may make the difference of vocational freedom or standard retirement, enjoying the fruits of your labor versus not being able to retire, and having to work to pay the expenses you have incurred.

Our casual desires cause many of us to make poor choices that are not mindful, causing us to chase material possessions, leaving little room if any to chase life's adventures. Save your hard-earned money for the things that truly bring you joy. Most material items and purchases are metabolized and experienced so quickly that many move onto their next purchases before savoring or finding any satisfaction in the things they bought. People end up valuing very little, because they neglect to take the time to appreciate experiences or reflect on what they have earned and worked hard to create. I see this trait in more kids than I wish to admit. Is it because they don't value the iPad you bought them because they didn't pay for it with their own money? Maybe; but maybe it is because our kids have come to expect this. The baseline our children have regarding how much is enough is much higher than it was when I was younger. This is societal and, if it continues, will break us as a nation and continue to divide us. Instead of accepting that they need these things, incorporate the *why, what,* and *how* into your discussions and maybe let them save and contribute to large purchases.

Money is a tool that allows us to embrace desires, and it grants us the freedom to realize our dreams—but only if we manage it properly. Money allows us to purchase our freedom. But if we pay only for today, we will have nothing for tomorrow. *If young adults don't pay themselves first, they rob themselves of a financially secure future.*

Whether you start with birthday checks or allowance money, teaching your children to save at least 10% of their earnings starting at a young age will help them make the practice of saving for tomorrow a habit.

Putting this concept into practice, when Jacob turned five, I bought him the classic Moonjar money bank. The Moonjar is divided into three parts: save, spend, and share. Every dollar he gets he divides into the three sections. I find the visualization of having three different places for dissemination of money helps to reinforce the very powerful lesson that money received is not intended solely to be spent.

Although Jacob is older now, we still use the Moonjar. Some of the savings we have moved into a savings and investment account, but the regular flow of money in still initially lands in the Moonjar in order to reinforce the lesson that you must not spend all that you receive. It does become a challenge now that many cash gifts are given by way of Amazon or Visa gift cards. In these cases, we have him calculate the total value of his gift cards and 30% of their value goes into his savings account while the remainder is left for him to spend and share. Often this involves an exchange of the gift card or Amazon card balance to me or Bernie while we swap the money in his savings account. There are apps that will buy your gift card for cash as well. The important component of this is that the child understands the value of what is received and then understands and builds a habit for where those dollars are going, no matter what form they come in.

In the wonderful book *Nudge* (Yale University Press, 2008), Richard Thaler shares the idea that only 5% of people are completely rational in their decision making. The remaining 95% of us need help thinking through our options before making decisions. Most of us often need help and support in order to do the right thing. In 2017, Thaler won a Nobel Prize in economics. Among his biggest successes was inspiring Congress to overhaul the nation's 401(k) system a decade earlier, working with organizations to create tools that help millions of individuals improve their chances for financial security. Thaler is one of the first to introduce the concept of automatic enrollment into retirement savings plans. Essentially, when you get a job at a company that offers a 401(k) plan, which is a retirement savings plan, you are automatically enrolled and as a result a percentage of your salary is taken out and put into the savings plan for you.

As of 2016, 58% of companies offering retirement plans provided auto-enrollment, and according to a study by Vanguard, auto-enrollment almost doubles employee participation, leading to higher savings rates for individuals. Auto-enrollment is the ultimate practice of "pay yourself first." A second important component of this practice is auto-escalation. This is the practice of increasing the percentage you save as your income increases. With auto-escalation, 401(k) plan participants automatically and incrementally increase contributions to their plans over time. Instead of obtaining a salary increase and automatically buying a bigger house or better car, increase the money you are saving so that you can build your wealth in order to enhance your personal economy.

Employing these two simple concepts can help create a generous foundation for wealth building at any age. It also shows that saving is a learned behavior. Many people, when given the choice, opt out of saving, either because they just don't think they can afford to, or they don't have a clear understanding of how savings will provide them with choice and freedom. It's not necessarily true that the more you save, the greater your wealth. It is true, however, that saving early and often provides you with the better chance to build wealth and live your life on purpose.

Study after study show that in the United States, we have learned poor savings habits. Our socialization processes have taught our culture that having stuff and money is great, but that money can also be a source of pain. Remember my inexact Facebook survey? Many people had very negative associations with it. Money, however, isn't the culprit, nor is it a matter of good versus evil. Rather, it is our actions, habits, and values that drive our choices and determine whether money will be a positive or negative force in our lives.

Other cultures and countries have a lot to teach us about the way we think of money. Even the way we speak about money may have a huge impact on our actions. Countries like China and Japan have radically different savings behaviors. A study by Keith Chen (TED, Feb. 2013), an associate professor of economics at UCLA–Anderson, provides evidence that these behaviors have everything to do with the language Chinese and Japanese investors use. The difference may lie in the difference between "future" and "futureless" languages. English speakers, for example, require information based on past, present, and future. We conjugate our verbs using tenses. Chinese, on the other hand, is a futureless language. To give you a better understanding, here is an example of the difference:

In English: "I *will* meet you in one hour."
In Chinese: "I meet you in one hour."

As a native English speaker, the second translation hurts my ears; however, this futureless language is not isolated to Chinese. It is similar in Japanese and Scandinavian countries.

What his study shows is that future-oriented languages like English—which divide past, present, and future—tend to disassociate the future from the present. This often leads English speakers to focus on the present without regard for the future while futureless languages speak about the present and future identically. Those languages that speak about the present and future identically tend to connect the past, present, and future—emotionally and financially. So, for those speaking futureless languages, saving for today is saving for tomorrow and there is no difference between your present and future self.

And the numbers support this theory. Families who equate the future with the present are 30% more likely to save and retire, ultimately ending up with 25% more savings than those who see the present and the future as separate entities.

One of the steps I discussed earlier in goal setting is Visualize. Visualizing our goals makes them real to us. Saving money as a goal works the same way. Consider a study that looked at two groups of employees who were signing up for their 401(k) plans. Half the employees saw digitally altered pictures of themselves at an older age on their signup forms. Those employees who saw images of their future selves saved more for their retirements. They were better able to bring the future to the present by visualizing and connecting emotionally to it.

Being mindful of how we speak about money, visualizing our goals and remembering that our money needs to support us, not only in the present but into the future, can help us adjust to develop better savings habits.

I recently came across something called Kakebo. Kakebo is the combination of three Japanese characters which literally translates to "book of accounts for household economy." The Japanese are big savers and believe that financial stability is a key factor for wellbeing. Kakebo dates to 1904, when a Japanese woman named Hani Motoki created a woman's magazine in which she urged readers to monitor their income and spending. Soon after, she published the first Kakebo, which was described as "a household accounting book designed to help ordinary people bring order to their finances in a mindful way."

The book follows a very similar process to budgeting, but instead of first looking at what is being spent, each month starts off thinking about how much you would like to save and what you need to do to accomplish this goal. During the month you write down your weekly spending and review at the end of each month. This is a very simple process and anyone can do it. At the end of each month you will have either fallen short of the savings goal, or not. There is space to reflect on the past months' successes, efforts, and failures, which may lead to changes you would need to incorporate into the future.

If we command our wealth, we shall be rich and free. If our wealth commands us, we are poor indeed.

—Edmund Burke

Most of us are creatures of habit, particularly the older we get. If we haven't had a budget or learned good savings habits, it is difficult to change. Starting kids saving early and often is the key to success. However, you can be a better saver at any age; it simply requires finding money to save. This could mean getting a side hustle, but it could also mean simply reducing expenses. Like Kakebo teaches us, set a savings goal at the beginning of each month and then simply track your spending. At the end of each month reflect upon your spending and look for areas to eliminate. We can gain a great deal by living with less. The chart shown here provides some ideas for saving:

Item	How often	Onetime expense	Monthly	Total cost savings over 25 years	Invested @ 5%
Latte	Daily	$5.00	$140.00	$42,000	$84,190
Netflix	Monthly	$10.99	$10.99	$3,297	$6,608
Lunch	Weekly	$20.00	$80.00	$24,000	$48,808

http://www.moneychimp.com/calculator/compound_interest_calculator.htm

In every scenario, saving money and then investing will more than double your money. Think about what you can do in 25 years with $84,000: perhaps fund a year of retirement, put a down payment on a beach house, or pay for college. There are so many meaningful options. Will you miss that daily latte in 25 years? I doubt it. It's all about defining what is important and taking the steps necessary to enhance your personal financial wellness.

I hope you will see that savings is not an option but a requirement to having your children live their best lives. How much should they save? The answer is different for everyone, but here are some guidelines.

How to Save

As we discussed with the advent of the automatic enrollment into a 401(k) plan, automation is the key for most.

1) *Set up a savings account.* You can either use your local bank and connect a savings account to your checking account at the same bank, or there are a number of online banks like Ally Bank or Capital One 360 that often provide a better interest rate for the savings.

2) *Establish a link.* When children are younger, have them give you their cash or checks or piggybank savings; you can deposit it into your checking account and then journal the money into their savings account. When children get older, they can establish their own direct deposit.

3) *Figure expenses.* What are your child's monthly expenses? This is an appropriate exercise typically around middle school when children branch out and become a bit more independent. This can be monthly movies, eating out, etc. This should become your child's personal budget.

4) *Save the balance.* Once children have a handle on what they spend monthly, they can save the rest.
5) *Monitor the results.* At least quarterly, review statements with your children. Knowledge is power.

Think of savings like buckets. The first bucket that must be filled is the "emergency" bucket. This is the cost of living for three to six months. For young children this can be the cost of going to the movies or getting ice cream; as children get older it could be gas money or eating out. This is your children's personal budget and should be money that can stay in their piggybank (think of the piggybank as the "checking account"). It may take several years for young children to build this up, but by the time they are age 10 or so, they should be ready for the next bucket. The next is the goals-based, long-term savings bucket. This will be time to go to the bank and open a savings account. Here, the 10 to 30% they save should automatically be put into this account. The money in this account should have a purpose. What is the child saving the money for? A new computer? A bike? A car? Shorter-term-goal purchases should be funded from the savings account. The specific goals your child has will dictate how much money to put in the account. Make sure the interest earned on the money in the account is competitive (check bankrate.com) and the fees are low to nothing. Once your children begin to earn income, at least 20% of what they earn should go directly into the savings account without a second thought. Eventually they will have three buckets of savings accounts:

Savings Account	Timeline	Purpose
Emergency Fund	Immediate	0–6 months of spending in case of an unforeseen emergency: loss of job, accident, new roof, etc.
Goals Based	1–10 years	Fund new purchases like a car or appliance; experiences like vacations, advanced degrees.
Freedom Fund	10 years and beyond	Vocational freedom, lifestyle

Technology has made our spending so easy and accessible that it is out of control with "invisible" money. But there are so many great apps and new ones popping up every day that make it so simple to save and these apps appeal to young people, more so than walking into a local branch "old school" to set up a savings account. Here are just a few:

Chime is an online bank app that has an automatic savings program as one of its main features.
Qapital is a hybrid automatic saving app that allows you to save based on goals.

Acorns is a hybrid investing and savings app that rounds up every purchase to the nearest dollar and invests the difference.

Tip Yourself is an app that allows you to transfer money from your checking account to your "tip jar."

There are so many ways to talk to kids about saving money. Here are some actionable steps to take with your kids and ways to get the conversation and good habits started.

Pre-K: Give your child a piggybank or Moonjar to allocate a portion of birthday and holiday money to their savings—at least 10%. When you go shopping with your kids, discuss discounts and savings on items purchased (and not purchased).

Elementary: Have your child continue to save, but this time make sure it is 10 to 30% of each amount they receive. Have them periodically count their savings. (Visualizing how money grows is critical for kids.) Take loose change and put it into a coin calculator or roll coins with your children. Get your child their first calculator.

Tweens: This is a great time to align your children's goals with their savings. Walk through the Planning with Purpose or the *why, what, how* steps and begin to incorporate it into their buying process. Use apps like Cardpool to sell gift cards for cash. Open a bank account for (and with) your kids and help them deposit their savings.

Teens: Review bank statements with your kids at least quarterly. Discuss fees, earned interest, etc. (See the section "Reading Your Investment Account Statements" in Chapter 10.) Get your child a debit card. Whether linked to their savings or funded from their savings, they need to begin to spend money now, as they will as adults. Help your kids track their spending and saving. Seeing where their money is going will give them opportunities to cut back and save (that weekly latte?). Any earned income from jobs should be saved in the bank account or a ROTH IRA.

College & Beyond: If your children have a 529 or other savings plan, or if you have committed to saving/investing a certain amount for college, make sure they understand any deficits that they are responsible for. Explicitly knowing what college will cost them will help them better plan, prepare, and save to pay off their debt. If they are offered a 401(k) plan with their first job, encourage them to invest 10% of their income and get the company match if there is a match available. This can and should be increased as their salaries increase until they are maxing out their contribution amounts. Discuss paying themselves first. Get apps like Acorns that turn spare change into savings.

Resources: moonjar.com, moneychimp.com savings calculators, Coin Counter, Green Light, Cardpool, Acorns.

Saving for College

It can be extremely overwhelming thinking about raising a child. One of the most overwhelming financial aspects of raising a child for Bernie and me was how in the world we were going to afford educating our child. I was lucky enough to work in the financial services industry and therefore had access to endless data about annual spending and college costs.

In 2016, the US Department of Agriculture (USDA) put out a study entitled, "The Cost of Expenditures by Family." It reasoned that the total cost of raising a child for 2015 was $233,610, varying depending on lifestyle, income, and number of children. We also found a nifty calculator that prompts you to enter your own specific data to come up with an annual figure. You can find it at CRC Calculator.

These numbers are eye-opening, but they do not even include college costs. As if day-to-day costs aren't scary enough, there are also college costs to consider. Through my research, I found that college costs had been increasing at an average rate of 7% each year (*Source:* "College Costs Are Soaring," *Inside Higher Ed,* October 2017) and weren't likely to slow down anytime soon.

Despite that Bernie and I both were solid earners, the thought of paying for a child and his college education terrified us. But what we discovered in our research illustrates the point of this chapter: the importance of saving, early and often.

The earlier you open a college savings account and automate saving every month for your child, the more prepared for those college costs you'll be. College is just one of the many goals you will need to save for over your lifetime and should be treated the exact same way. Each college savings plan has different minimums, penalties, and benefits that should be considered, and it's important to not get scared off by the details. In many cases, the minimum amount needed to open an account is only $100.

So, if you decide college or post-secondary education is worth it for your child, how will you save and pay for it? The good news is there are several ways. It's important to evaluate the nuances of each to determine how effective they can be at helping you meet your college-savings goals. Here are just a few to consider:

529 Plan account: The 529 was named after Section 529 in the Internal Revenue Code adopted in 1996, which allowed states or educational institutions to create college savings programs for families. A benefit of these plans is that dollars contributed can be withdrawn tax-free as long as they are used for *qualified educational expenses*. There are many other benefits to 529 plans for college-bound children, but all plans are not created equal. The good news is that you are not limited by state. Most 529 plans, regardless of your residency, are open and available to you. Some states provide tax credits while 31 states allow income tax deductions against annual contributions. Other states don't cap annual deductions, but cap deductions against the lifetime contributions for each child. Lucky for Bernie and me, South Carolina currently offers one of the highest deductions at $370,000. Additionally, South Carolina's plan is considered "direct-sold," meaning it is sold directly to residents and as a result has some of the lowest costs nationally. A major disadvantage to a 529 plan is that if you withdraw funds in excess of your *qualified education expenses* (i.e. for a purpose other than education), the IRS will assess a 10% withdrawal penalty on these funds. If earnings are included in the total, you will have to pay regular income tax on them as well. *Bottom line:* Great for the college-bound child, but don't overfund these accounts in case your child does not end up in college. *Tip:* Always use the direct-sold plan, not an advisor plan, as these plans are simple and there is no need to pay an advisor a fee. There was a recent change in the law which allows money from a 529 plan to also be used to fund K-12 tuition, up to $10,000 per child.

Uniform Gift to Minors/Uniform Transfer to Minors (UGMA/UTMA) account: UGMA/UTMA accounts provide a way for families to save on behalf of a minor child without setting up a trust fund. One of the key advantages of these accounts is flexibility; you can put a large range of investment options inside a UGMA/UTMA, including stocks and mutual funds, creating a custom portfolio designed to meet the child's unique investment goals. When funds are withdrawn, their use is not limited to qualified educational expenses. The funds may be used as the donor or child (upon the age of majority) sees fit, and there are no contribution limits. The assets become the child's property when he or she reaches the age of the majority (18 or 21, depending on state of residence). This is a potential drawback, because it leaves the donor with no real control over how the money is spent. The second is that for college-bound children, substantial UGMA/UTMA assets can tend to work against them in financial-aid calculations. Finally, the money gifted to the child is irrevocable. *Bottom line:* Great for an investor who wishes to make an irrevocable gift of securities or cash to a minor.

Coverdell Educations Savings Account/Educational IRA: This account is an educational savings vehicle for families looking to save for college *and* K–12 education. Like the UGMA/UTMA, this vehicle offers flexibility of investment choices. Like the 529, dollars withdrawn are tax-free if the proceeds are used for qualified educational expenses (inclusive of K–12). There are, however, some unique features of the Coverdell ESA: maximum investment per beneficiary is $2,000 per year, contributions must end by age 18, and the child must use the assets by age 30. *Bottom line:* Great option for families saving for K–12 private education; savings strategy can be combined with 529.

When planning for education, or any life event, it's important to consider an appropriate balance of fees, state and federal income-tax savings, as well as your return on investment.

A great resource for all things college-savings-related is the website www .savingforcollege.com.

Debt

I distinctly remember sitting in an executive committee meeting in my late twenties listening to the CFO of our company discuss our P&L and company Balance Sheet. To be honest, most of the discussion was difficult for me to follow. He started in on the assets and liabilities of the firm, and it is at this moment that I reframed my thinking around debt. While discussing our firm's substantial liabilities (debt), which was met with a palpable groan, our CEO quickly jumped in and explained that the debt was primarily due to the acquisition we just made of a new firm; he explained simply, "This is good debt." I thought, *Huh?* Isn't *good debt* an oxymoron? I had always associated debt as bad. Debt was only for those things someone couldn't afford—credit cards, student loans, home loans, car loans, and so on. What is to distinguish good from bad?

Here I was working in the financial services field and honestly had no idea what he was talking about. Without thinking, I asked, "What do you mean by *good* debt?" Thank goodness for the leadership he exhibited. Instead of making me feel like uneducated fool for asking such a question in an executive forum, he went on to explain simply: "Good debt is debt that you take on in order to generate additional income and increase your wealth." He went on to explain that as a company we had the option of paying for the new firm outright, cleaning out most of our cash and investment position, or taking on debt for the purchase. (I always assumed if you have the money to pay for the thing, you pay for it!) He continued that after running the numbers it was clear that even with the cost of the debt repayments, we were projected to increase our revenue growth rates by over 20% each year. Additionally, we enjoyed tax benefits by taking on the debt and were able to keep our other money free and working for us instead of being tied up in buying the other firm.

The biggest lesson this taught me about making purchasing decisions is to always think about debt in terms of making an investment. It is necessary to evaluate all your options and do the math. What will the purchase cost, including fees and interest, and what will the expected return be? Here the business we acquired was not only able to pay off the debt, it added income to our business. From a personal standpoint the idea of buying a home and taking on debt is typical. Most don't think of it this way, but each debt payment we make is exchanged for equity in the home. I consider this as good debt; your payments are made toward an asset that will most likely increase in value if you hold onto the house for a long enough period of time. Consider buying a car: Is this good or bad debt? How about putting a vacation or a new pair of shoes on credit? Bad debt is borrowed money used to make lifestyle acquisitions, like the car, the vacation, or the shoes. These are items that tend to decrease in value as soon as you buy them; they most likely will not generate an income stream (unless you are an Uber driver!).

Student Loan Debt—Good or Bad?

What about the 1.5 trillion—yes, *trillion*—dollars of student loan debt? Is this good or bad debt? The answer is, it depends! An education is certainly an investment in oneself, but at what price?

First, let's start with a general picture of the student loan landscape. The most recent reports indicate:

- $1.56 trillion in total US student loan debt
- 44.7 million Americans with student loan debt
- 11.5% of student loans that are 90 days or more delinquent or are in default
- Average monthly student loan payment (among those not in deferment): $393
- Median monthly student loan payment (among those not in deferment): $222

(*Source:* Data from the US Federal Reserve and the Federal Reserve Bank of New York.)

Of the $1.56 trillion in student loan debt, a trillion dollars of the debt was added between 2006 and 2018 and continues to grow. There has been much debate recently about whether higher education, and more specifically, the cost of a traditional four-year college education, is worth it. College tuition has soared 1,375% since 1978, more than four times the rate of overall inflation, Labor Department data show. That's more than healthcare and gas price increases *combined*. With these burgeoning costs, it's logical to ask whether the cost of college is a worthy investment.

How did we get here? During the 1960s, at the time of the Lyndon Johnson Administration, it became clear that college could help individuals grow their human and financial capital and indirectly help to grow the economy. The administration wanted to provide everyone the opportunity to attend college, no matter their financial circumstance, and so they created a panel, led by economist Alice Rivlin, to determine how all individuals could gain access to higher education. In 1972, President Nixon put into place the Higher Education Act, mostly following the Rivlin panel recommendations, direct loans from private banks made to students that are government guaranteed. Think of the government as the co-signor for students who had no credit or resources of their own.

There were unforeseen consequences, not the least of which was that many students who took out loans never completed college and simply didn't have the resources to pay the loans. There was also little oversight; colleges began to lower their entrance standards and increase their tuition rates simply because they knew that the federal government was on the hook for paying the tuition, no matter what happened with the student. The Obama Administration, in an effort to fix the broken system, cut out the middleman (private banks) and took on all student loan debt. The Department of Education became, essentially, a bank. Here we are today, and the intent of the Johnson Administration has largely been met—a large majority of the population has earned a college degree and this has help grow our economy. Ironically, the unforeseen consequences of this very admirable goal are proving to have the potential to destroy both the personal and collective economy of the United States and its citizens.

Now here we are with astronomical increases in college prices, many saddled with debt, putting our future leaders at a supreme disadvantage that certainly does not leave them feeling financially well. In addition to the statistics for students, their parents who have taken out loans for them are also suffering. It was recently reported by CBS News that 40,000 over the age of 65 are having their Social Security payments, tax refunds, or other government payments garnished because of the student loan debt they simply can't afford to pay. Imagine entering your retirement years with student debt! We are beginning to witness the long-term impact of this with young people delaying getting married, buying a home, and having children (we have the lowest birthrate in over 32 years). This not only delays many young adults from acquiring assets and raising families, it also tends to delay their ability to save for retirement, not to mention their ability to do things that will help stimulate economic growth for the rest of us.

There are, of course, certain obvious positive effects of obtaining a college degree. From an investment standpoint, obtaining a college degree will lead to more pay. A recent study by Pew Research found that the earnings divide between college graduates and high school graduates is particularly wide in the current Millennial generation. In 1979, high school graduates of the Baby Boomer generation earned about 75% of what their college-educated peers did. Today, Millennial high school graduates bring in just 62 cents on the dollar compared to their college-educated peers. As education increases, so, too, does one's earning potential.

It is also shown that obtaining a college degree can lead to steadier employment. Additionally, obtaining better-paying jobs tends to open employees up to better benefits. According to a 2016 College Board report, 54% of full-time workers with a high school diploma had employer-related health insurance while 70% of advanced-degree holders had employer-provided health insurance. Not to mention the intangibles of going to college, like expanding one's network, creating lifelong friendships, opening one's mind to new experiences, and generally learning to live independently.

Yet while the majority of kids today seem to be conditioned to attend college, each of us is unique with our own set of skills and abilities. Consider what your own children will need to become financially well. What type of degree or experience will best fuel their passion? It may no longer be about how much money they can make with a degree, but about what a degree will cost them in time and money, and whether that degree will enable them to live their life's purpose.

If college is in your child's future, the next question, before he or she starts looking at schools, is *how much can we afford?*

College costs: According to LendingTree, in 2019 the average cost of a public in-state college is $25,290. These numbers are the national average and can easily quadruple for out-of-state or private schools. Run your own numbers and share them with your student. This is your child's investment, not yours. Help them understand it in a way that is tangible to them.

- What is the cost of skipping one class in a 15-week semester? About $70. That's a week's worth of pizza slices.
- What is the cost of failing a class? $3,000! That's real money to an 18-year-old (and to me). Compare this to the cost of spending that spring break in the Caribbean or at home sleeping in their old room that was converted to a media room.

Just remember that none of this information is meant or should be used to scare or cause kids anxiety about the college experience. It is simply meant to help them engage in a higher level of thinking when it comes to not only their field of study, but also their financial decisions, because college truly is an investment in *themselves*, and if they decide to skip class or not put in the effort, they need to understand the financial implications of doing so.

A lucky few will have enough money in their 529 or trust accounts to cover the cost of college. However, most will need to consider taking out student loans. This is the point in the journey where your children need to engage in the discussion about "investing" in college, and the cost of doing so. Back to good debt versus bad debt: student loans can be considered good debt. Your children are making an investment in themselves—an investment that will increase their future salary. Sounds fabulous, where do I sign?

Not so fast!

Understand the true cost of student debt. Most kids will leave school with debt and they should be aware of exactly what this looks like. Will they be responsible for $250 per month or $1,000 per month student loan repayment? We have made it so easy for kids to gain access to student loans, but we do them a great disservice by not explaining that their decisions have consequences, sometimes decades-long consequences. What does an extra semester cost in terms of future repayments? Will my current major and its future job prospects provide enough income for me to pay back my loan and support myself? Among the Class of 2018, 69% of college students took out student loans and they graduated with an average debt of $29,800.

The monthly payment on a $29,800 student loan is approximately $323 (assuming 5.5% interest and a 10-year repayment plan), which can cause financial strain if you're not prepared for it. At the end of the 10-year period, your student will have paid back the principal plus $9,009 in interest for a total of $38,809. It is imperative that your children understand the total impact of that loan (studentloanhero.com has a series of calculators to help you with this discussion).

A great rule of thumb is to limit student loan debt to 10% or less of your after-tax monthly income. If your child had a loan of $29,800, she would have to land a job for around $56,000 per year in order to keep her payments at 10% or less of her salary. Assuming an after-tax salary of $3,266 per month (30% taken out for taxes and 401(k) savings), she could afford $326 a month. According to College Pulse Survey, the median salary in 2018 for a college graduate with between zero and five years' experience is $48,400. Naturally, location of the job and the actual job itself would dictate if your student would fall on the higher or lower end of the salary. Don't wait until after college and after the loans are already taken out to have this conversation.

A Simple Exercise (Example):

1) Add up your resources:
   Financial Resources for College
   - 529/College Savings: $40,000
   - Additional money from parents: $15,000
   - Other resources: $5,000

   Total Financial Resources: $60,000

2) Understand your potential for income:
   Anticipated Major: Education
   Average Starting Salary: $37,000

3) Calculate your acceptable student loan debt:
   Total Student Loan Debt Calculation
   a) (Average Starting Salary * .70)/12 = monthly income
      $$($37,000*.70)/12) = \$2,158$$
   b) Monthly Income * .10 = acceptable monthly payment
      $$($2,158 * .10) = \$215.83$$
   c) Go to financial-calculators.com/loan calculator:
      a) Enter number of payments: 120 (10 years).
      b) Enter interest rate (here I used 5.5%).
      c) Monthly Payment = $215.83.

      Enter Calculate
      Total Acceptable Student Loan Debt = $19,887

4) Add together your Total Financial Resources and your Acceptable Student Loan Debt to understand how much you can afford to pay for your college investment:

$$\$60,000 + \$19,887 = \$79,887$$

Now, talk to a college counselor about your options, potential merit money or grants, evaluate your choices, and then pick a college.

Money-Minded Motivation

- ✔ *Pay yourself first.*
- ✔ Money is just a thing; never make the mistake of giving it your power.
- ✔ Make saving *automatic*.
- ✔ Introduce the concept of a budget to your children as soon as they begin to spend.
- ✔ When your children are faced with taking on debt, calculate what they can actually afford and understand the length of time they will carry the debt.
- ✔ Limit student loan debt to 10% or less of your after-tax monthly income.

8

Principles of Money Management: Spend

Financial resources should be used as a means toward achieving self-actualization. If you want to evaluate your priorities, take a look at your checkbook. Does your spending align with your values?

Conscious spending requires an understanding of what is important to you, controlling cash, and living in a place of self-sufficiency. Developing this conscious understanding and clarity not only helps to remove the emotions from financial decision making, but also prevents mindless spending, which often leads to a negative net worth and bad debt. Teaching our kids to plan their spending from a young age will help them become financially well later in life.

Consider that we teach our children math in the classroom, yet they often don't know how to apply the concepts in their daily lives. How many times have your children asked *why* they need to do their math problems? I realized when Jacob was young that while he learned math skills well, he was not able to apply the skills in real life. Schoolteachers can only do so much. Enter our role as parents in the real world.

To help Jacob apply his math skills in daily life, I try to make buying experiences a lesson on budgeting and finance. Tween and teen years are a great time to start these lessons.

When Jacob was 11, we took a holiday trip to Mt. Tremblant and Montreal, Canada. As a family, we decided that our financial and personal resources are better spent doing things together instead of buying things to celebrate holidays. This does not mean we don't get suckered into buying things while on holiday. In fact, my husband and son may have more t-shirts and baseball caps than most sporting goods stores!

Bernie and I have found it was helpful to teach Jacob to plan and research our trips with us, and to determine together what types of things we'd all like to do while on vacation. Our Canada trip included a Montreal Canadiens game and, while researching the trip, we learned that hockey tickets in Canada are just about as pricey as NFL football tickets in the States. But knowing that, we were able to plan ahead and prioritize some of our spending.

One fun lesson that happened on our visit came from the combination of Boxing Day, a Canadian shopping day holiday, and the conversion of the Canadian dollar (the loon, which I learned is the country's bird). Boxing Day sale discounts, combined with the dollar conversion, created lots of math lessons and price comparisons for Jacob at age 11. And honestly, this challenged us all.

First, we had to find each item's price, then understand the "solde" or sale discount—typically 20 to 50% off—and then convert that amount into the US dollar. Fortunately, we were on the favorable side of the equation. During our stay in Québec, the Canadian dollar was 0.80 to the US dollar. We kept saying, "Everything is 20% off! *Yay!*"

While it took a few tries, Jacob caught on to the conversion process pretty quickly. There were, of course, a few cries of, "Mommy, I am on vacation! I am not in school—why do I have to do math?" However, the grumbling quickly subsided when I said, "No math, no (insert item desired by 11-year-old boy, i.e. hockey puck, Expos t-shirt, Kinder Surprise Eggs, etc.)."

Teaching our kids to apply their math skills is unquestionably a lot of *work* and it's often met with resistance, but it is essential to helping our children grow. We, as parents and caregivers, work tirelessly, repeating, reinforcing, and nagging to an exhausting limit that sometimes leaves us feeling empty. But then, there are moments, albeit brief, when our child exemplifies what we have been inculcating into their lives since birth. These moments that are difficult to describe, but we all know them when we see them. It's the feelings we get when we see our children walk, speak, and experience life with confidence and without intimidation. This confidence is only learned through experience and guidance/mentoring—financial wellness is much the same.

It's clear that we can't count on schools to teach our children everything there is to know about fiscal responsibility. The curriculum in most, if not all, states includes a wide variety of math topics, but little on the topics of applying that math to real-life scenarios. Personal financial management skills, things like creating a simple budget and balancing online bank statements, are rarely taught. While many states introduce children in the fourth grade to the "stock market game," it is both short-term and focused primarily on stock market performance. To me, this is like putting the cart before the horse.

There are infinite ways to start teaching our kids, especially our teens, spending skills. When you go out to dinner, ask them to guess how much the bill will be. This will help them practice basic addition, as well as an understanding of the cost of goods. Next, ask them to figure out the tip. Here they will use their multiplication, decimal, and percentage skills. When you are shopping and something is on sale, do the same thing. This will help them reinforce lessons at school and it will quickly become second nature to apply these skills in their everyday lives.

Spending money can be fun and very productive when spending is well-planned and uses common sense. This means doing research before making major purchases and waiting for the right time to buy.

A key component in smart spending is knowing what you can afford. This seems simple enough, but how many people do you know who "run out of money" at the end of the month? Sadly, many people turn to credit cards or other types of borrowing when they run out of money to meet their needs. Keeping in mind that while some debt is "good debt," like a reasonable mortgage you have the ability to pay off, most debt creates a sense of powerlessness. Having an awareness of what you own, what you owe, what you earn, and where your money is going creates conscious spending and helps eliminate the risk of running out of money. The last thing we want out children to do when they get money is to spend it all. Once your children begin to "earn" money, from any source, it is time to introduce a process to help them identify their "personal balance sheet" (PBS), which we discuss in the next section. To bring this awareness to light I recommend you start with a simple budget or spending survey.

The Ins and Outs of Budgeting

In the previous chapter we discussed Kakebo, the idea that we start with what we will save each month and then evaluate our success. Think of budgeting as a tool for creating awareness. Any budget or spending survey will include these two simple categories: in and out. As we get older these categories become a bit more granular, but at any age, these two categories will work. It's all about what's coming in and what's going out. It's that simple.

Let's focus on the *in* first.

When kids are young, the *ins* are generally minimal and include things like gifts and allowances, if there are any. As your child gets older, the ins may also include things like dividends or interest on their savings accounts. For most people who enter the workforce, salary, bonus, and commissions become the primary source of ins. Financial responsibility means your ins should *always* be more than your outs!

Similarly, *outs* begin very simply and then grow exponentially as we get older. The challenge for most people is that the possibilities for ins are much more limited than the seemingly endless outs. When kids are young, the outs are simple, limited to things like entertainment, movies, jump zones, or discretionary items like toys, iPads, and so forth. As we grow older and responsible for ourselves, the outs grow into basic needs such as clothing, food, automobiles, housing, and insurance. Anything that costs money within the month is an out. This includes savings.

When children are younger, they should have a good handle, at least annually, on their personal balance sheet (PBS). This includes ins, outs, and balances in any "bank," whether piggybank or otherwise. This will help them plan. Just keep in mind, this isn't meant to be perfect or a time hog. It is simply meant to paint a picture of your monthly or annual spending and savings, giving you and your children clarity and providing areas for improvement.

Again, technology makes our lives a bit easier when it comes to tracking our spending, not just facilitating our spending. Once your child begins to use a debit card, simply review their account statements to help them track spending or link to an online tracking tool which will help to categorize spending and make your child aware of their good and bad spending habits.

How Much Should I Save If I Want $1 Million?

How to Save $1,000,000 by Age 65

Amount saved	$0 (PV on financial calculator)
Amount we want to have saved by 65	$1,000,000 (FV on financial calculator)
Annualized market return expectation	7% per year (I on financial calculator)
Years until 65	40 (N on financial calculator)
Years' contribution to 401(k) required	$5,009 (PMT on financial calculator)
Dollar amount contribution per paycheck required	$209 ($5,009/24)

(*Source:* Karen Wallace, Morningstar, 8-14-2018.)

When kids go off to college, it's especially important that they know how to budget. College is the time to engage in new experiences and personal growth. For most kids, it's their first time living away from home, free to make their own choices. As parents, we tend to enforce the importance of making smart academic and social choices, but we also need to include financial choices as part of our discussions with our kids.

Living away from home requires kids to figure out when and what to eat, how much to spend on the party this weekend, or whether they can afford the trip to see the big away football game. College is the perfect time for kids to learn about making sound financial choices. But they also need to be prepared to make those choices consciously.

They should know how much they spend and what they are spending it on. This sounds so simple, but remember, most kids have never been fully responsible for funding their own bank accounts or accountable for the way their money is spent.

This is a great introduction. Ask them to create a monthly budget for food or treats, clothes, entertainment, and an emergency fund. Whether you as a parent are funding their accounts or not, have the children do the work to figure out how much they need—and then hold them accountable. Running out of money to buy the things they want and need is a great way to open their eyes and set realistic expectations, and to reinforce the importance of having a budget. They can go online and create a budget on mint.com, and if they don't do it, you can set one up for them. Each month, they can review their spending habits and patterns. Ninety-nine times out of 100, they will blow through their budget, but this is a time for learning and experimenting.

I recently read a blog by David Ramsey, who is the master at simplifying spending. He discusses four bad habits each of us needs to break in order to lead to better spending. And remember, our children learn just as much from our intentional teachings as they do from our unintentional lessons. First, never spend without a plan. We have discussed this at length: without a plan we all tend to go off the reservation; a plan helps to keep us focused and disciplined. Dave Ramsey suggests giving every dollar a name. That is to say, give every dollar a purpose. It's harder to spend a dollar named "college savings" on a pair of shoes you don't really need.

Next, he says to stop regularly paying for convenience. For example, eating out every night because it's just easier and quicker. If you plan your meals at the beginning of the week, you have created your own convenience and will save money.

Third, don't make the mistake of not tracking your money. We have discussed this at length, and it is so foundational that I will mention it again. Clarity leads to power and power leads to change and freedom.

Finally, stay away from impulse purchases. If you give every dollar a name, this will be less likely to occur, but sometimes we are just weak, especially after a long day with our children. If you have a "pocket-money" category, says Dave Ramsey, when it runs out so, too, does the ability to make an impulse purchase. The empty pocket-money account or envelope will reinforce all of the good habits you are working to develop in both yourself and your child. Keeping an open dialogue about how you are managing your spending and why is also critical to your child's financial wellness.

Whoever said money can't buy happiness simply didn't know where to go shopping.

—Bo Derek

While this quote from Bo is very amusing, think about it: Can money really buy happiness? If so, what can you or your children purchase that will make you happy? An experiment done by Tom Gilovich tested this hypothesis—can money really make you happy? He had his subjects draw a big empty circle and then around the big circle, a series of smaller circles with recent large purchases they made over the last few months. Large purchases were $100 or more.

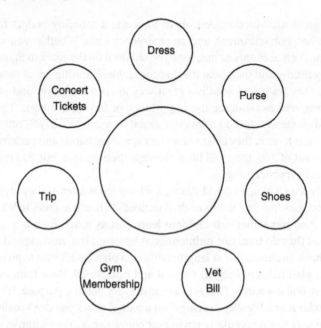

Next, he asked his subjects to replicate the large circle and write "Values" in the middle of the circle. Then, redraw each of the smaller circles and place them on or near the Values circle based on how closely they align with your personal Values. Those on the circle perfectly align; those away from the circle do not. Like this:

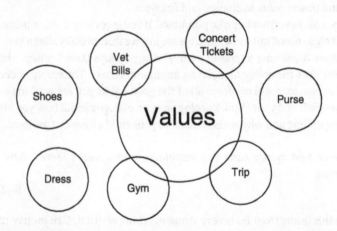

What he found was that most "experiential" purchases were those mostly aligned with an individual's values—trips to explore new places, vacations with families, concerts, ballets, movies, and so on. Things that aren't tangible were the most aligned with values and presumably happiness.

This can be a fun exercise to run through with your children. When they review their monthly spending, they can follow a similar exercise. Presumably "pizza" or "latte" will appear as a frequent item. This is a good time to review the "cost of the latte" or pizza or whatever to show them that delaying satisfaction today could lead to a larger purchase that not only will align with their values but will provide them with a truly invaluable experience. Have your kids *dream big*. Let them know that with discipline and dedication anything is possible.

Another tip to control excessive spending is to have a weekly "spend day." How many of our Amazon shopping carts are filled with items for our "save for later" list? Delaying purchases puts time and space between your decision and your purchase and allows you and your child time to reflect and really consider whether they want to spend their money on such a thing. I often use Friday as my spend day. I will review my Amazon or other lists to see what I thought I needed to have throughout the week and inevitably will refine my purchases down to a few items that I believe are necessary or that I want, or end up spending nothing at all. This exercise brings to light how frivolous many of our purchases are and, honestly, when I review my save-for-later items I often find myself laughing at some of them. Imagine we simply pulled the trigger every time we were a sucker for click-bait or some other marketing scam. Many of us do exactly that and we must learn to control these impulses by putting time and clarity between our purchases.

Credit Cards

Just say "No!" Credit can be good. You often need to have credit, in particular "good credit," in order to buy something; however, good debt can turn bad very quickly if you use your credit card and build up a balance of debt. Debt can often be impossible to crawl out of. Let your kids know that those shiny toys the credit card companies are giving away are not worth their future borrowing capacity. In college your kids will be presented with numerous offers from different credit card companies: free tickets, free t-shirts, pop-sockets, and so on. This is a scam. These companies try to entice students to open cards when they have no meaningful source of income to pay off the cards. This is why 80% of graduating college seniors have credit card debt. The mindset of buy-now-pay-later is a recipe for disaster and one that will damage your credit and your future savings potential. Now, I do advocate having a credit card, but you should purchase only what you can afford to pay off at the end of the month. There are lots of options with points and travel rewards, and all of these are great, but they are not a reason to own a credit card if you don't have the discipline to pay the balance off each month. When the time is right, your children can do the research to determine which credit card suits them best. Here are a few scary numbers you can share with them.

According to creditcards.com, the average rate of credit card interest is just under 17%. If you carry an average daily balance of $3,000 in credit card debt, your minimum payment will be around $50 a month. If the credit card charges a 17% APR, the interest could cost you over $500 per year.

Here's how to figure it out:

1) Divide your APR by 365 days per year: 17% / 365 = (about) 0.0465%.
2) Multiply 0.0465% by 30 days per month: 0.0465% × 30 = 1.3, or .013%.
3) Multiply 0.013% by the $3,000 original balance = $41.00 a month in interest.

Or you can use the bankrate.com calculator:

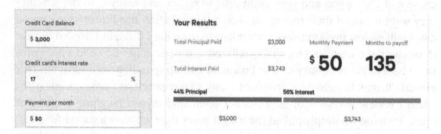

With a $50 minimum payment, it will take more than 11 years to pay off the purchase—over a decade! Chances are what you bought will be outdated, outmoded, lost, or broken by then. This is a great exercise to help kids understand the full costs of their purchases. An informed consumer is a smart consumer.

What happens if you miss a payment or carry too much of a balance? Well, these things will affect your credit rating. And as I mentioned, a good credit rating is necessary to your positive financial wellness, for instance, securing a loan for a home or car and when doing so getting the best possible interest rate. A bad credit rating will cause you to pay even more on the loan (i.e. a higher interest rate) than someone with a good credit rating, costing you potentially thousands of dollars over your lifetime. Additionally, when you go to rent an apartment or even apply for a job, credit ratings are used to evaluate your ability to pay and evaluate your reliability as an employee. So, a good lesson to take is that one silly credit card you signed up for as a junior in college could have far-reaching negative impacts on your future self and your ability to reach financial wellness. Just say *no*. If you can't afford it, save for it until you can or do without.

Here is how to help your kids to make smart spending decisions:

Pre-K: Teach your kids to differentiate between *needs* versus *wants*, a critical skill to master at this age. This will help to remove emotion from financial decision making.

For example, when your kids want things, instead of rewarding them with instant gratification by making quick purchases, encourage them to do their research. Kids are no strangers to technology, and this is the perfect opportunity to teach them to do some invaluable research online. Show them how to check for value, quality, warranty, price comparisons, and consumer reviews. Have them research items before buying. This will accomplish one of two things: it will either quash their interest in the item and make their want fade away, or it will help them acquire information to make smart, informed decisions about their purchases. If they continue to want the item, this is a great time to introduce them to a simple budget tool.

Elementary: Continue to reinforce needs versus wants. Children often have, at this age, accumulated some savings and will begin to think more independently about spending money. Have them bring a few of their own dollars when going to the movies or the store to make purchases independently of you. This will give them a direct accountability in spending their dollars, not yours. After all, it's much easier to spend someone else's money.

Tweens: By this age your children should have some math skills under their belt that you can help them apply in the real world. Have your children calculate the tip when you go out. If you travel to a destination with a different currency, have them convert the currency. When they want something, teach them how to comparison shop. Teach them patience in purchasing, and that sometimes good things are worth waiting for.

Teens: Teens have very busy and expensive lifestyles. Everything starts to get bigger and costlier during the teen years. Here it is critical to introduce values into the way your child spends money. It is also a time where you can't continue to fund every desire and whim your child has, and you are likely to have lots of heated discussions around this topic. "Everyone else is doing it," will start to sound familiar. If your child "wants it all," he can prioritize how important things are by working, earning, and spending his own income. Between academics and extracurricular activities, kids these days don't have much time; but if something is truly important for them to have and you have decided not to fund it, they can either become resourceful and find a way or decide it wasn't that important. Providing your children a "budget" of what you will give them each month will set their expectations and help them manage what and how they spend.

College & Beyond: If you are providing some financial support during the college years, continue helping with a budget and identifying what you will provide to your children each month. Between your support and their own earnings, tools like mint.com can be a helpful resource. At some point during college, getting a job is important, and not just to pad the resume. Spending earned money can put a whole new lens on purchases (similar to the "life energy" Joe Dominguez discusses in his book, *Your Money or Your Life*). This can be a hard lesson in spending within means. Early adult years can provide difficult life lessons in spending, budgeting, and the value of money if kids aren't prepared. Credit cards may enter the pictures as a quick and easy way to access money. College loans may also enter the picture. (Read above regarding what your decisions cost.) Yet a child saddled with debt and poor spending habits is in for a stress-filled, unhappy, financially unwell future, and it's up to you to help them avoid this scenario.

Resources: cash register, college calculators, consumer resources, budgeting software, mint.com.

Some of the most substantial items most children will spend money on are cars, college, and a home. We previously discussed college; let's look at other major purchases here.

Cars

My very first car was a Volvo that I bought from my boss's wife. I was just about to graduate from college and needed a car of my own. I worked part-time waitressing on the weekends and without much thought when he said she was getting rid of the car, I said "Sure, I'll buy it." It was a beautiful car, too big for me, but had a huge sunroof and gorgeous leather seats. I had the car for less than two years when I realized what it cost to fix a foreign car. I could barely afford my rent and would soon have to live in the car unless I made a change. Over the years I have leased cars, purchased cars, leased and then purchased a car, bought new, certified preowned, and so on. What I have learned is that it is important to do the math. I wrote previously about looking at big purchases as an investment. A car, unless it is a classic, really isn't an investment; it is more like an appliance, necessary for most but not something that will increase in value. Most cars once they come off the lot automatically decrease in value significantly.

In order to avoid my many mistakes, encourage your children to go into buying a car, like any investment, with a plan. Here are a few good considerations:

1) How will I use the car?
   a) How many miles a month will I drive?
   b) Long distance, short distance?
   c) What is important to have in the car/truck? A third row?
   d) What technology do I prefer/need? (These add-ons can be expensive; remember your smartphone can handle most if not all these bells and whistles.)
2) What can I afford?
   a) Understand this *before* you go car shopping. Have a very specific budget in mind.

b) Remember, this isn't just what you can afford per month. Many dealers will extend the terms of your financing up to six years, lowering your monthly payment but increasing the total car payments. *Example:* If you are looking at a $25,000 car at 5% interest:

Term	Monthly Cost	Total Cost
48	$576	$27,635
72	$403	$28,989

Most people look at the lower monthly payment and say as I did, "I'll take it!" But the monthly figures are misleading. Taking the lower monthly payment also extends the time you will have to pay for an additional 24 months or two years. And your total payments over time are higher.

Good practice suggests that when buying a car you should put down at least 20%, you should finance the car for no more than four years, and you should keep your monthly car payment (including your principal, interest, insurance, and other expenses) at or below 10% of your gross monthly income.

c) Once you determine what you can afford, you will need to secure financing. Keep in mind that you don't have to get financing through the car dealership. Very often you can obtain a personal loan directly from a bank for a lower interest rate.

3) How long will I keep the car?

a) If you plan to keep the car less than three years, leasing is probably a better option.

b) Leasing makes sense if you drive less than 12,000 miles a year (or less than your lease permits), you plan to keep the car for a short period of time, and you want the cost of maintenance covered.

c) Buying is more expensive than leasing in the short term. The typical break-even on buying a car versus leasing is about five years. So, if you plan to keep your car for at least five years, buy it.

4) Do your research:

a) Buying new? Look for dealer incentives on their websites.

b) Buying used? There are several online used-car sites that will help you get a feel for pricing, options, makes and models, and general price range.

c) If you have a trade-in, know its value. *Kelly Blue Book* is still the go-to source for this.

5) Save for a down payment. Whether you buy or lease, you will have to pay something upfront to get the car.

Buying a House

Of all the changes we have seen from our parents' generation, and even for those of us over 40, buying a house is by far the biggest shift in perspective. We so often focus on the question of whether the cost of college is worth it, and many just assume buying a home is the natural order of things. Frankly, that idea is outdated. I spoke previously about "good debt," and taking out a mortgage to buy a house is always at the top of the list of the good-debt pile, but a lot has changed. As parents, let's take the pressure off the gas a little and understand that the traditional path we took may not be viable or even desirable for our children. Think about the idea of paying yourself first. Many homeowners can't afford to do this because most of their money goes into paying their mortgage debt. They are what we refer to as "house-poor." And with the large student loan debt many young adults are saddled with today, how in the world can they then come up with 20% to put down on the house? The question young adults are often faced with is "Should I rent or buy?"

Following are some guidelines to consider.

How Long?

Buying a home versus renting is very similar to the discussion about buying a car. A good first question to ask is how long you plan to stay in the house.

The cost of buying a home includes upfront expenses like brokers' fees, title insurance, appraisals, and so on. Depending where you live you may have additional costs that you did not anticipate, like flood insurance or hurricane insurance. Once you have found an ideal location, work with a realtor to understand the nuances and additional financial requirements the location requires. Many planned communities also have HOAs or Home Ownership Association fees which can be very costly. In addition, if you get a mortgage, most of what you are paying in the early years is mostly interest on the loan; your payments have barely touched the principal, which means what you borrowed and what you owe in a few short years may be very similar. So, if you are only planning to stay in the house a few years, the upfront expenses may outweigh your sales price, causing you to simply break even or even lose money on the transaction. Remember, home prices don't always go up, especially in the short run.

What Can I Afford?

1) Make sure you have at least 20% to put down on a house before you even think about looking. Without 20% down you will be required to pay something called "PMI" insurance. Essentially, PMI is insurance the lenders require someone pay, on top of their mortgage payment, in case of default. The conventional

thinking is that if someone cannot come up with a 20% down payment for the house, they may not be able to afford the monthly mortgage payments. There are ways to avoid PMI and for individuals with significant assets, and experience buying homes, this is worth looking into; however, for a first-time home buyer, make sure you have 20% to put down on a home.

2) When looking for a mortgage a good place to find the best rates is LendingTree or Credible. This will give you a good framework for how much your monthly payments will be. Most lenders will look at something called your debt-to-income ratio. The debt-to-income ratio is calculated by adding up all your monthly *debt* payments and dividing them by your gross monthly *income*. Your gross monthly *income* is generally the amount of money you have earned before your taxes and other deductions are taken out. Most lenders require this ratio not be higher than 43%.

Salary of $50,000 equates to a max monthly payment of $1,791.
This assumes your child has no other debt and puts 20% down.
If your child has other debt, say a $500 student loan, her max payment would be $1,291 ($1,791 – other debt of $500).

A best practice when buying a home is to keep your debt-to-income ratio at 30% or less. Doing this will help you build equity in your home and save more toward your future.

3) Consider the costs of owning a home. There will be regular maintenance on the home, purchases for the home, and if the home is older, unforeseen repairs. Many budgeting experts suggest you will pay an additional 1% of the cost of the home annually on repairs and maintenance.

4) Writing off the interest. You may hear some people say it's always better to own a home because you can "write off" the mortgage interest. Recent tax law changes have removed the interest deduction, so this is no longer a reason to buy a home.

Renting a House

What Can I Afford?

The budgetary guidelines suggest not spending more than 30% of your net income on rent. Personally, if you want to save money toward future goals, including financial freedom, I would recommend not spending more than 20% of your net pay on rent. Depending on the location where your child lives and their salary, owning a home may simply not be an option. Living in larger cities, particularly those on the coasts, it may be very difficult to rent a place for less than 40% of their net take-home pay. Spending 40% of one's take-home is never advisable unless there will be an extreme pickup in salary within a few years that will reduce their rental payment percentage closer to 20%.

Evaluating Renting versus Buying

Even if your child has the money, buying isn't always the best way to go. Aside from only staying in the house a few short years, the location of where your child will live will color their decision to buy or rent. Another good rule of thumb is to look at the *price-to-rent ratio*, which is the *price of the property/rent*.

Realtor.com has a great calculator that will detail the costs of renting versus buying monthly. It also includes when the breakeven will be, that is, when it makes sense financially to buy or rent. In the example below, assume your child is looking at either buying a home costing $400,000 or a monthly budget allowing for rent of $1,600. You will see that *after* 6 years, buying becomes the more prudent option. At year 6, the initial costs have been paid and they will be at breakeven. Each year after year 6, the decision to buy versus rent serves to increase the value of the asset.

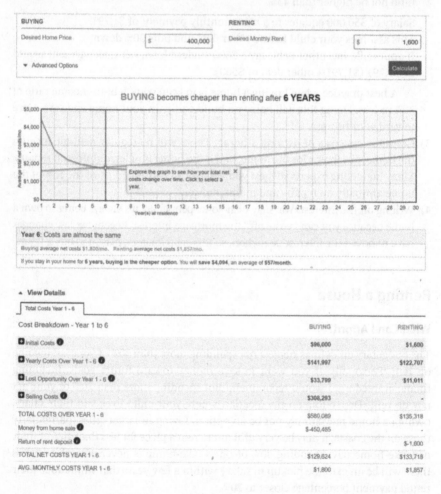

Cost Breakdown - Year 1 to 6	BUYING	RENTING
Initial Costs	$96,000	$1,600
Yearly Costs Over Year 1 - 6	$141,997	$122,707
Lost Opportunity Over Year 1 - 6	$33,799	$11,011
Selling Costs	$308,293	-
TOTAL COSTS OVER YEAR 1 - 6	$580,089	$135,318
Money from home sale	$-450,485	-
Return of rent deposit	-	$-1,600
TOTAL NET COSTS YEAR 1 - 6	$129,824	$133,718
AVG. MONTHLY COSTS YEAR 1 - 6	$1,800	$1,857

The bottom line is that buying a home is no longer a rite of passage or the American Dream. Buying a home must be a thoughtful, mindful exercise whose results will be unique to your child's situation. As their income and circumstances change, the decision to rent or buy should be reevaluated.

Skin in the Game

I've talked a great deal about the shift in perspective that must take place in order to lead our children along the path of financial wellness. I am going to be a bit provocative here and say that it is not just our perspective about how we think, talk, and socialize around money, but it is our parenting methods that need to also change. Just like our own habits with money, our parenting methods were also learned and developed from what we experienced growing up. Most of us grew up in a time where it was better to be seen and not heard, where we simply ate what was served or we went hungry. Developing a healthy relationship for money with your children requires us to shift from this hierarchical parental role where we as parents are always in control to one in which we are influencers of our children's behavior. Giving our children a voice instead of simply dictating the way it will be helps to engage them and make them part of the process. Keep in mind that giving someone a voice is not the same as turning over your authority.

At the beginning of the book I mentioned *entitlement*, as in the way the younger generations have come to feel that if they want something, they expect their parents to procure it for them immediately no matter the cost. This teaches children to think, "If I want something, someone will give it to me." And we all know that in the real world this is not how things work. When children have a false sense of entitlement, by the time they are adults they believe their parents, and everyone else for that matter, "owe" them whatever they want. We are stressed beyond reason as parents and we often feel guilty about working too much, not being home for dinner, missing the competition, or not volunteering enough in your child's school (the list is endless), so we often cope by giving them things to compensate for our absence. This is *normal*; don't beat yourself up about it. Just recognize what you are doing and understand the implication.

Consider that if we give our kids whatever they want, they do in fact become entitled; they believe we and the world around them owe them things. Entering adulthood with this mindset is a recipe for failure, both as a successful member of society and to be financially well. Let me be clear, I am not saying it is a bad thing to buy your children things. But I do believe that the *way* you give them things creates certain expectations—either of entitlement or of a sense of ownership and pride.

Jacob joined the JV football team this past fall, and for any sports parents out there, you know joining sports teams comes with a pricetag. Even when your kids play for school, they need a certain amount of equipment. Playing JV football as a seventh-grader is a major time, physical, and emotional commitment that he was taking on, and we were proud of him. We rewarded his determination and his effort by buying him all the gear he needed. Halfway into the season, while walking off the field at a game, Jacob lost his left-handed receiver's glove. I didn't find out until we got in the car and asked why he was wandering around the field after the game. "My glove fell off my helmet when I was shaking hands, and someone must have picked it up; it's gone." My response, "I am sorry that you lost your glove, but they were $40 gloves and you are going to have to do without, or just wear one." Wearing just one glove was clearly mortifying, as was the idea of not having gloves, so the next day he called me after school and asked me if I would take him to get new gloves and that he had a coupon from Dick's Sporting Goods and had the money to pay for them. This made me smile. He knew that, yes, I can afford to buy him a new pair of gloves, but he also understands the concept of ownership. He was not entitled to the second pair of gloves, in fact he wasn't entitled to the first pair of gloves; we purchased them as a reward for his commitment to such a challenging undertaking. Attach your values to your purchases and communicate them to your child.

Let's talk about things a little bigger than a pair of football gloves. We have previously discussed big purchases your child will undertake: college, car, and home. If you can pay for some or all of these big-ticket items for your child, consider the *way* you do it. You have several options other than writing a check for the entire amount.

You have heard the saying "skin in the game." Essentially, a person with skin in the game has a personal stake in the desired outcome. We need our kids to have some skin in the game when it comes to paying for all or a portion of their major purchases. The first step is to talk to them about these things, early and often. Let them have both a voice and a personal stake in the outcome. Your values and their values will become apparent during this process. Here are a few options to consider.

The first is what I call the back-end buck. I have heard a great many horror stories where parents save and pay for their children to go to a great school but after year 1, 2, or 3 their child decides to drop out or is kicked out. As a parent you have just paid out thousands and thousands of your hard-earned dollars that you can't recoup, and your child has no college degree to show for it. Now, expecting your child to pay for college tuition and room and board is quite difficult. First, they are limited to the total amount of federal student loans they can get and simply don't have the capacity to earn enough before or during school to cover the costs. One solution I have seen more recently is when parents want to pay for their child's education but are unsure if their child is a good fit, the parent will take out loans for the amount of the education and *if* they finish school, the parents will pay back all or a large portion of those loans. *If* the child does not complete their education, the child is on the hook to pay back the loans. Parents have this conversation up front and their child understands that if they don't pursue their degree, they will owe a certain amount monthly, or if they finish school, the amount will be much lower or nothing. They have skin in the game to finish their degree or perhaps even decide while having the conversation that college is in fact not for them. Kids need to be part of the decision-making process on such matters that impact their future.

The second option is the incentive approach. Consider purchasing a car. If your child is set on getting a car at age 16, instead of just handing them a new car, incent them to save by matching their investment in the car. They can start saving their gift money or from jobs. Let them know that you will match dollar for dollar what they save to get their new car. If your child is not able to earn money to cover the cost of the car due to lack of jobs for their age or time to work, before buying the car tell them they are responsible for the car's carrying costs. They will need enough money saved to cover the cost of insurance and gas for the first year and will be responsible for those costs thereafter. Let them know this is not a free ride; they need to understand responsibility, and this is a good time to introduce them to car insurance and the potential financial cost of getting in an accident. For college-bound students if the back-end buck doesn't work for you, you can tell your children that you will pay for their education, but they are on the hook for all other costs: books, food, entertainment, and so on. I have even seen parents create "incentive" language in their Trusts for the money they will be leaving to their children. This language provides expectations that their children must exhibit in order to get money from the Trust. For example, the Trust will distribute $1 for every $1 the child earns.

Get creative with your children. You know what drives them and what will inspire them to take ownership in their outcomes. Keep in mind, every child is different, and some are more inherently aware of their skin in the game, but others are not. You may need different approaches for different children, so talk to them, make them part of the process. The important thing for parents to do is to articulate what you value and what you want your child to learn and communicate this message, early and often, when dealing with financial purchases. These are all foundational, teachable moments that will lead to your child's financial success.

Underlying the skin in the game idea is the value of hard work, grit, and earning things. Children need to see the integral connection between making an effort and achieving success. Next we look at *how to earn*.

Earning Money

At some point the well runs dry for spending and the birthday checks and holiday gift cards simply aren't enough to fund your child's personal budget. What many parents will do is to simply "fund the gap." They will hand out $20 bills left and right to fund their children's lifestyle—lifestyles that are getting more and more expensive by the day. When I was 12 years old, I baby-sat all summer and had a paper route with my brother. I often look back and wonder how in the world someone left me with two young children to watch eight hours a day when I was only 12 years old, but I did it and made lots of money. Every summer after that I worked at the swim club and during the school year I would work at a bakery or some other retail outlet. If I wanted or needed something, I worked for it and bought it. In addition to working I also played two sports, made good grades, and was very social. Our children live in a different world today. If your child plays sports or is into the arts, their practice, games, and performances consume a great deal of their free time. There is very little, if any, time left for them to work at a traditional job. There are, however, other options to teach kids about earning their own money that don't require your child to get a traditional job.

First, consider giving them an allowance. Yes, the money is still coming from you, but you could attach certain requirements to their receiving the allowance. Some people don't agree with giving a child an allowance while others give an allowance but don't expect any work to be attached to it. No matter your stance, if you provide an allowance to your child, make sure they treat it the same way as any other source of income, saving and spending mindfully.

The Girl Scouts and Boy Scouts of America provide wonderful lessons on earning money and general financial literacy. If you can expose your children to one of these programs, they will most certainly have a strong foundation on how to earn and manage money. If physically attending meetings or working is not an option for your child, once again technology provides lots of opportunities for our children to make money. There are several sites that allow kids to buy and sell goods. eBay was the original but many more specialized sites have popped up. A favorite of Jacob's is StockX, where he can sell sneakers or other sportswear items. Kids make money from YouTube videos, Instagram, and so on. I am not endorsing any of these, but the opportunities are out there, and I challenge you and your children to find a way to have them earn their own money.

Hard work is hard work no matter the platform. Working all summer is not an option for all kids; the lessons that working provides can also be found in playing sports, acting school, and so on, but there is very little that can replace earning your own paycheck. Help your children find a way to earn some money of their own. I have seen firsthand the confidence and satisfaction children derive from earning their first paycheck.

Taxes

One can't discuss earning money without discussing paying taxes. When we discuss *net* versus *gross* pay, we are mainly saying that what you earn before taxes = gross pay, and what you take home after taxes = net pay.

Paycheck

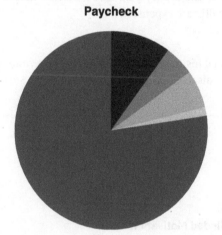

■ Fed ■ State ■ Social Sec ■ Medicare ■ Take Home

As shown in the image, the following taxes are taken out of your hard-earned money:

- Federal Taxes @ 10% (assume the lowest tax bracket for young workers)
- State Taxes @ 5% (each state is different)
- Social Security @ 6.2%
- Medicare @ 1.45%

If your child earned a gross pay of $1,000, their net or take-home pay, after taxes, would be $773.60.

When your child begins to pay into a 401(k) or other retirement plan, these dollars also come out of the gross figure, thereby reducing further the net or take-home pay.

Since your children will be paying over 20% of their earned income to taxes, I think it is important for them to understand what their taxes do.

Federal Taxes

Federal taxes pay for government employees, freeways and highways that cross state lines, wars, the military, and so forth.

State Taxes

State taxes pay for state employees, public schools, local roads, state funded programs, and so on.

Medicare Taxes

When you are over 65 a portion of the money paid into Medicare will be given back to you to cover certain healthcare expenses.

Social Security Taxes

Social Security taxes go to the social insurance program that the government uses to help support people who are disabled or retired.

Money-Minded Motivation

- ✔ Richness comes from your soul, spirit, character, and values.
- ✔ Mindful spending is spending that aligns with your values; try the exercise Can Money Make you Happy? with your child.
- ✔ Spend less; search more.
- ✔ Earning money is the key to success.
- ✔ Make sure your children understand how to earn and the implications of taxes and other expenses for their paycheck.
- ✔ Before making a major purchase, have your children do the research to understand what they can truly afford.

9

Principles of Money Management: Share

Sharing is one of the most fundamental lessons we teach toddlers, encouraged at schools and in the broader community. As parents, we can all recall cringeworthy moments when our children had temper tantrums, screamed at the top of their lungs, or even bit other children, all because someone had something they wanted. Most of us quickly intervene, encouraging our children to share and apologizing profusely to those around us while we turn crimson red with embarrassment.

We are taught that sharing is caring, yet for many of us somewhere along the way sharing becomes less important. In fact, sharing becomes obsolete. When, how, why does it happen? It certainly isn't something we consciously decide. We just stop putting so much emphasis on it as we shift from sharing with others to trying to keep up with others. We attach less value to sharing and more value to "getting," the more complicated our social and emotional lives become. Unfortunately, because many of us stop focusing on sharing as our children age, our children often lose sight of its importance and their role in helping others. Somewhere along the way we trade sharing for competing, and with having and needing more than everyone else. This is called consumerism because it literally consumes us. To combat it, we need to reweave the privilege of sharing into our children's lives and help shift their perspective.

No matter our religious, social, political, or other leanings, most people I encounter are very giving and have generous hearts. However, I often find that people wait until they are older, middle-aged to retired, before they begin to be charitable. After losing our early connection to sharing, it can take us decades to return to placing importance on sharing with our communities, economy, and our world in general. This is perhaps because *wanting* to help and provide for others and the causes we care about isn't enough—it requires money and time and sacrifice.

To be clear, I make no presumptions offering any specific rules or judgments on what you and your family share or don't share. What we share or don't share is very personal. Very often, like our spending and saving habits, sharing is aligned with values. We support what we value. We offer our time and money to those causes that are most meaningful to us.

You and your children can prioritize your charitable giving alongside your other goals as part of your budget. Teaching and showing your children, early and often, how and when to be charitable is very important for so many reasons.

Separate from money, we all have time and talent to share with others. Being charitable doesn't necessarily mean you need to spend thousands of dollars a year on a particular cause. It does, however, mean being conscious of what is important to you, your family, and community and using the resources you have in order to help your cause. Causes are unique to each individual, but nonetheless, it's important to demonstrate to your children why giving and sharing our resources are vital to contributing to a healthier world.

Here are some statistics about giving from the Blackbaud Institute's 2018 Charitable Giving Report:

- Overall charitable giving in the United States has increased 1.5% on a year-over-year basis. Since 2016, overall giving has grown 9%.
- Online giving grew 1.2% in 2018. Since 2016, online giving has grown 17% and average online gift amounts have continued to increase. The average online donation in 2018 was $147.
- Approximately 8.5% of overall fundraising revenue, excluding grants, was raised online in 2018—another record high.
- In 2018, 24% of online transactions were made using a mobile device.
- December remains the largest giving month of the year with 17% of overall giving and 17.3% of online giving for the year.

Our giving overall continues to steadily increase. Technology, again, is making it easier and easier for us to give, but it is also making it easier for us to give mindlessly. How many times have you clicked a crowdfunding link for a child with cancer or a donate button from a Facebook page showing a dog in need of medical care? To be money-minded means that we are using our finances to express our family's core values *and* each dollar must have a purpose. Is your giving bucket full or empty? Do you know what percentage of your income you allocate to a sharing cause?

This fable can help remind us and teach our children that no matter who we are, we all need a little help sometimes and sharing with others is what makes the word go around.

The Giraffe and the Monkeys

From the land of Africa comes a most unusual story. A big giraffe came upon a family of very happy monkeys that were living in a valley of fruit trees. The giraffe, being quite tall, began eating fruit off the top of one tree that was as high as a house.

"Please, sir, don't eat all of our fruit," said a monkey in the tree. "We would be happy to share many different kinds of fruit with you, if you will share with us."

"What do you mean by the word *share*?" asked the giraffe.

"I'll explain," said the monkey. "This tree is a pear tree. But the family next to us lives in an orange tree. And the family next to them lives in a plum tree. We give some of our fruit to them, and they share some of their fruit with us. That way, everyone is happy."

"Oh, that's not so smart," said the giraffe. "What if you don't have anything to give to them? Do they still give to you?"

"Of course they do, because friends share with friends," said the monkey.

"It may be good for you monkeys," replied the giraffe, "but not for me. I am the tallest animal in the world, and I shall continue to share with myself." And off he went, eating more leaves and fruit.

But something frightening was coming. That evening, a powerful rainstorm blew over the valley, and there were flashes of lightning and claps of thunder everywhere. The giraffe tried to hide under the tallest tree. But as he stepped under it, a bolt of lightning struck the tree.

A big branch suddenly fell from above and landed on the giraffe's head and neck, knocking him to the ground. He didn't move for a long time. And when the storm finally blew away, he slowly woke up. But something terrible had happened. He could not raise his long neck. When he stood up, his head was hanging to the ground.

Several monkeys saw what had happened and came down. "You are in big trouble, Mister Giraffe. How are you going to eat fruit and leaves from the tops of trees?"

"I don't know," replied the giraffe. "Please, can't you and your friends help me?"

"No, I'm sorry," said one of the monkeys. "We have rules. We can share our food only with those who share with us."

"But what am I to do?" cried the giraffe.

"I don't know," answered the monkey, "but when you get hungry, I am sure you will think of something." And the monkeys went back into the tree.

It wasn't long before the giraffe was hungry. But what could he eat? He only saw berry bushes along the ground, and the berries were too small for his mouth. Then he suddenly thought of something, just as the monkey said he

(Continued)

The Giraffe and the Monkeys (Continued)

would. He picked up all the berries he could find and carried them to the bottom of the tree where the monkeys lived. He then looked up and shouted: "Hey, monkeys, can we be friends? I've brought something nice to share with you."

Several monkeys came down and tasted the berries. "Oh, thank you, Mister Giraffe, these berries taste good. You have made us very happy."

"Gee," said the giraffe, "I've never made anyone happy before—except myself."

"Well," replied one of the monkeys, "now you know how it feels to make someone else happy." And with that, the monkeys quickly ran up the tree and began throwing fruit and fresh leaves to the ground. Before he could count to ten, there was more food on the ground than the giraffe could eat.

Time passed by, and the giraffe's neck became well. He could once again eat leaves from the tops of trees. But he decided to stay in the valley near the monkeys and share many meals together, *because sharing is what living is all about.*

When you share aplenty, your rewards are many.

(Source: African fable, author unknown.)

Monkeys and giraffes aren't all that different from us. There is actual evidence that giving money away not only benefits others, but it can lead to increased happiness for the sharer himself. In a popular TED Talk from 2011, Michael Norton, a professor of Business Administration at the Harvard Business School, spoke about money and happiness.

On a Vancouver morning, we went out on the campus at University of British Columbia, approached people and said, "Do you want to be in an experiment?" They said, "Yes." We asked them how happy they were, and then gave them an envelope with money. One of the envelopes had things in it that said, "By 5 p.m. today, spend this money on yourself." We gave some examples of what you could spend it on. Other people got a slip of paper that said, "By 5 p.m. today, spend this money on somebody else."

And we manipulated how much money we gave them; some people got this slip of paper and five dollars; some got this slip of paper and twenty dollars. We let them go about their day and do whatever they wanted. We found out they did spend it in the way we asked them to. We called them up and asked them, "What did you spend it on? How happy do you feel now?" What did they spend it on? These are college undergrads; a lot of what they spent it on for themselves were things like earrings and makeup. One woman said she bought a stuffed animal for her niece. People gave money to homeless people.

So, if you give undergraduates five dollars, it looks like coffee to them, and they run over to Starbucks and spend it as fast as they can. Some people bought coffee for themselves, the way they usually would, but others bought coffee for somebody else. So, the very same purchase, just targeted toward yourself or targeted toward somebody else. What did we find when we called at the end of the day? People who spent money on others got happier; people who spent it on themselves, nothing happened. It didn't make them less happy; it just didn't do much for them.

In a more recent scientific study published in *Nature Communications*, researchers from the University of Zurich, Switzerland, told 50 people they'd be receiving about $100 over a few weeks. Half of the people were asked to commit to spending that money on themselves, and half were asked to spend it on someone they knew. Participants who spent money on others made more generous choices in an independent decision-making task and showed stronger increases in self-reported happiness.

We make a living by what we get, but we make a life by what we give.
—Winston Churchill

And of course, there are tax and other financial incentives to being charitable, investing in low-income communities, helping with revitalization efforts, and so forth. They say it is always better to give than to receive, but with a charitable donation you are both giving and receiving at the same time. Here are a few things to consider with your planned giving.

First and foremost, make it planned, that is, have a plan for your giving. We talk a great deal in this book about every dollar having a purpose; your charitable dollars should also have a purpose. This requires you to be proactive in your giving, to identify the causes and things that are important to you and your family. Do you wish to give to families in need, animal welfare, international relief efforts, or environmental groups? Decide which one or many causes you would like to support. Next, do your research. Make sure the charity is designated as a 501c(3) by the IRS; this is the barebones standard of a charity and does not mean they are legitimate. Every year these companies are required to file a Form 990; this form lists the firm's financial information. It is here that you can gain an understanding of the companies' overhead costs, donations, and how much of their donations are actually going to the cause you are wishing to support. These forms are not simple to evaluate and decipher, which is why I recommend using a third party to evaluate the best charitable organization to fit your funding goals. There are several independent watchdog groups that rank and review charities, like Charitablenavigator.org, the Better Business Bureau, Consumer Reports rankings, and Guidestar.org, to name a few. These companies will advise if 90 cents of every dollar you give goes to the charity or toward overhead.

Next consider how you give. Are you giving cash, securities, goods, or a vehicle? Each has a different potential tax benefit. Do you itemize or take the standard deduction on your taxes? You should know the answer to this so you know if your charitable giving actually does provide you with a tax benefit. When tax brackets and laws change, you will need to ask your CPA how these may impact your giving and adjust accordingly.

Finally, track your investment. Giving to a charity is a form of investment. You are investing in the cause, the research, and the people administering the charity. Are they getting the results you had hoped for? Are they doing what they say they are doing? The sea of charitable giving seems to be growing by the day, so do your homework, keep an eye open for new ways to give, and understand both the altruistic and financial benefits of your gift.

As a visual person, I like to think of sharing as the flower that blooms from our financial wellbeing, the gift of gratitude that we can give to others. No matter the size of your bank account or stock portfolio, giving and sharing your time, intellect, or money with others and seeing how your efforts lift them up is part of your life's energy.

Again, how your share your money and time is a personal decision but teaching your children to help support those things that are important to them is a valuable lesson that will help them grow emotionally, seeing the world as bigger than themselves. Here are some ways to start the discussions at various ages:

Pre-K: Explain your sharing to your child. Bring them along when you are sharing your time, talents, or treasures. Set the example of how to share.

Elementary: At this age, your child is old enough to have some preferences for causes of their own to support. Have them select a charity or cause that is meaningful to them and have them donate time or money—the amount is of no importance; the action is what is important. For example, have your child go through their outgrown toys or clothes and have them donate to those less fortunate, or ask them to write letters to servicemen, or volunteer at an animal shelter.

Tweens: Have your child participate in a community service project. Many schools require or offer options for your children to participate in volunteer or service projects. Discuss with your children how giving their time has impacted others; help them make a habit of regularly donating their time.

Teens: If your child has a special talent, have them use it to help others. Perhaps they could, for example, tutor or teach music. Giving their time to others and seeing the impact it has can be powerful for their self-esteem and sense of purpose. At this stage, your child is probably passionate about a few things (not just other teens!), and this is a good time to introduce financial charitable giving. Have them research different organizations, learn how the money is being spent, whom it serves, and how their donations can help advance the cause.

College & Beyond: Sharing and gifting are often used interchangeably in the financial world. A college education, funded in part or in full by someone else, is one of the biggest gifts our children will ever receive. Make sure they understand and identify this as a true gift if they have received it. Continue to encourage your children to support that which fuels their passion. Our communities depend on volunteerism, donations of items, and talents. This is a lifelong quest.

Money-Minded Motivation

- ✓ Find your passion and use your personal resources to help fulfill it.
- ✓ Philanthropy provides a wonderful platform for educating the next generation as to family dynamics, the importance of giving money away, and the role of outside advisors.
- ✓ What you appreciate, appreciates.
- ✓ Give with intention and do your research.

10

Principles of Money Management: Invest

A good investment can increase the quality of your life.

In this section, we will focus on some foundational investment concepts that you and your children can build upon. Most of us cannot accumulate the amount of money we will need to support our short-term and long-term goals by saving alone. This makes investing necessary to reach our financial goals. The good news is that the toughest lessons to learn about managing money are how to save and how to spend on a budget, which you and your child have already mastered if you have made it this far into the book. Once your child understands how to mindfully save, spend, and hopefully earn money, it's time to put those skills into practice by helping them learn how to invest. Investing, in simple terms, is a way to make your money work for you. This is the path to building wealth and, more importantly, to securing a comfortable financial future for your children.

Proper investing and planning focus on the long term. So, children younger than age 10 will probably have a difficult time grasping the idea of investing, simply because the future is too elusive a concept at that age. With younger children, you can start to introduce the idea of investing by discussing how investing time and effort into things improves results. For example, you can use this example when planting and watering seeds and waiting for the flowers to bloom, mixing ingredients and waiting patiently for the sweet cake, or working hard on a puzzle or Lego set and enjoying the result. These are all good foundational examples that reinforce the basics of investing. With effort and time, along with a dose of patience, you will see growth in their understanding of the concept of investing.

For children older than 10, or even young adults just starting out, you can begin to build on these basics. The first question that most people and children ask is: I am ready to invest, what should I buy? By this they usually mean, should I buy specific stocks such as Facebook or Apple or whatever the highest-performing, most media-worthy stock is at the time. Elementary- and middle-school-aged children can start with stock picking. Picking stocks, while not the "best" way to invest, can help kids engage in the process of investing by learning how to research companies, to understand what a stock is, to buy it, and to gain an appreciation for market risks.

I don't have a crystal ball to lend you that will help predict whether a company will gain or lose money, but we can do research to help understand more about different companies and their prospects. I like young children to think about investing in the companies they know and use. This makes it real for them, and hopefully fun, too. The first stocks that Jacob bought were Microsoft (he owns a Chromebook loaded with Microsoft product), Nike (he is a sneaker fanatic), Dick's Sporting Goods (where most of his discretionary money goes), and Facebook (he is not on Facebook, but thought it was a great investment because it was trading so high). Share with your children that when you buy stock in a company, you become a partial "owner" of that company. That is a big deal to a kid! Here is a simple definition of a stock you can share with them:

> **Stock:** Public companies raise money by selling shares of their company (stock) to investors. If you own stock, you're a *partial owner* of the company, and as an owner, you're entitled to a portion of the company's profits. In general, stocks have higher levels of risk than other types of investments and will most likely result in higher gains (more money) over time. The tradeoff is that in the shorter term the stock may be volatile, creating a series of ups and downs (chance of losing money).

Before actually taking your children's savings and opening an investment account to buy stocks, I recommend they play around a bit with stock research first. There are several great apps and online research tools you can introduce to them to learn about stocks and even make and track hypothetical investments. YAHOO! Finance is a free website that offers resources to research stocks. Here is a screenshot of Facebook stock on YAHOO! Finance:

You often will hear "Buy low, sell high," meaning you ideally want to buy a stock at a low price with the hopes that it will rise and you can then sell it when it is priced higher and earn a profit. This sounds great, but again, every day brings a different set of price movements or volatility in the stock price, so this strategy is generally only smart as a long-term strategy. Doing proper research will help you to gain a better understanding of where the stock is today compared to where it has been, to help evaluate if the stock is relatively cheap (low) or relatively expensive (high).

I have highlighted a few items on the Facebook stock quote to help you gain a better understanding of stock price and how much a stock will cost relative to its historical prices (high or low). Performance alone doesn't tell the entire story. Below the chart (but not shown here) you will typically see a series of recent news articles about the company. These articles can help your child understand if there is positive or negative information available about the company, some of which they may already

1. Listed first is the price. Here, $144.24 is the price the moment this was captured on January 23, 2019, at 12:22.
2. The first line in the chart, the previous close, shows what the company stock price was the prior day.
3. The change +/– appears next to the price. Here the stock price is down –3.33.
4. The chart to the right shows the ups/downs of the price over 1 day, 5 days, 1 month, 1 year, etc. This helps you see the price volatility or risk.
5. The 52-week range shows where the stock price has been over the past year and helps you to evaluate if the price today falls at the high or low end of that price.

know if they are active users of the company or have seen it in the news. Typically, companies that have negative news may not have great future earnings or potential for growth while companies with positive information may be good to buy on hopes that the good news will increase the stock's price. Some other research items to consider: Is the company profitable (i.e. making money)? Is the company growing into new markets and hiring people or have they recently let go of staff? Does the company have a competitive advantage? While this is a very simplistic way to view a company's potential for growth, it's a great way for newbie investors to get started.

Many other websites also have free tools that allow your children to set up mock investment portfolios and track stocks' progress. Google, YAHOO!, and Morningstar have great websites with tools that allow you to create model investment portfolios. There are also many apps that make investing in stocks an adventure. Tracking each investment and following the ups and downs of the market will help your child gain a better understanding of how the markets work.

One of the most important concepts for your child to understand before investing is the concept of risk. Understanding what level of risk your child is comfortable with is important. When we refer to *risk* in this context, we are also referring to how much the buyer is willing to lose. Which company in Jacob's starter portfolio took a fall first? You guessed it, Facebook. Soon after he purchased Facebook, a rash of negative information about both the company's privacy controls and future earnings surfaced and caused the stock price to fall. While by most accounts Facebook is a solid company with a unique product that will most likely pay off for him in the long term; in the short term he learned about volatility, or short-term price fluctuations, as we discussed earlier. Fortunately, not all of Jacob's money was invested in Facebook. He spread his money across a few different stocks, and this is called *diversification*.

The game Whack-a-Mole from many years ago can be used as an analogy for kids to understand diversification. In Whack-a-Mole, moles pop up and down from their holes at random and the object is to whack the moles back down while more moles simultaneously pop up. In investing, if you diversify or spread your investment dollars across different types of companies, when one stock inevitably gets hit and "goes down," another may pop up at the same time, balancing out your investment return. This diversification helps to reduce the risk that everything will get hit and go down at once. Similarly, what are the risks of getting all green candies in a bag of Skittles? Relatively low, right? When you open a bag of Skittles and toss the candy on the table you see a rainbow of colors. Think of your investments this way—you want lots of different types in order to achieve a balanced portfolio that will help you reach your long-term goals.

Once your children have researched different types of companies, watched the ups and downs of a mock portfolio, and understands the potential risks, then they are ready to open their own investment accounts with their *own* money! Every parent needs to use their judgment to decide when their own child is ready to move to this next step. Opening an account and investing in the stock market does bear risks, as we have discussed, and this means your children could lose money. If they are not properly prepared, they could lose all their money, like I did right out of college when I put all my money into two stocks that both crashed and burned.

Though I am now a financial advisor, it took me years to learn and hone some of these simple lessons and unlearn some bad habits. I hope that by sharing the following story with you, you will understand the importance of teaching children at a young age, early and often, the discipline of investing. Here is the story of how I lost all my money when I was 22 years old (and working in the financial profession!):

> I learned the lesson of the importance of diversification the hard way. When I was first out of college, working for Merrill Lynch, I started dabbling with investing for the first time during the late-1990s tech craze, or the dot-com bubble as it is now known. I put all my hard-earned money into two stocks— Worldcom.com and Pets.com—in my 401(k) account. How I invested my

money was the exact opposite of diversification and is called holding concentrated positions. My entire account was concentrated in two new technology companies, companies with very little information available to research and evaluate. I not only invested all my money in stocks but invested it in just two stocks in the same industry. Talk about taking on excessive risk! I did not consider risk or diversification but just chased what I thought would bring the highest returns. I had no plan, except perhaps a "get-rich-quick" plan. This was a foolhardy way to invest. Both companies I invested all my money in eventually imploded and went out of business, bringing the value of both companies, and my stocks, down to $0.

Bottom line: don't rush into investing or chase performance. This is called *speculating*, not investing. Investing should not be a short-term game, but rather a long-term journey.

Once you determine your children are ready to move money from their savings account to an investment account, there are a few other bits of information that are important for them to learn. The first is that you'll need to select a custodian or company online with whom to open the account. You don't need to hire a financial advisor to facilitate purchasing stock; however, if you work with a financial advisor whom you trust, you can certainly reach out to them and ask if they will accommodate your child's account. Otherwise, you have several options. There are many different low-cost online companies with low minimums where you can open an investment account on behalf of your child. Companies like Vanguard, E*TRADE, TDAmeritrade, or my favorite, Charles Schwab, as well as a plethora of others can be good options to get started. Many allow you to go online and open the account within a few short minutes; some will even allow you to transfer money directly from your bank account on the spot. Make sure the cost to open the account and the cost to buy and sell stocks is low.

What these firms facilitate on your behalf is the buying and selling of stock from the stock exchanges, where the companies are listed. When you think of a stock exchange, picture a farmers' market where each vendor at the market represents a different company. The manager of the farmers' market allows and approves the vendors to sell their wares at the market. People come from all over to buy products from these vendors. The stock exchange operates on the same concept, where vendors are companies and people from all over the world buy and sell their stock. Opening an investment account is your virtual entry into the market.

Through an online investing company like E*TRADE, TDAmeritrade, or Vanguard, or your advisor, you and your child can pick companies to buy, identify how much you want to invest in each company, and simply click enter. Your order will then be sent to the market to purchase the stock. The market routes the order to the stock exchange where that company is held. The most notable stock exchanges in the United States are the New York Stock Exchange (NYSE) and the NASDAQ.

The NYSE is the largest stock exchange. It hosts some of the largest companies in the United States and has the most trading activity of all stock exchanges in the world. The NASDAQ is the second-largest exchange and primarily hosts large technology companies.

Since most stocks trade throughout the day, your order will be executed immediately and you will see the money in your investment account exchanged for shares of the companies you purchased. Typically, you will receive monthly account statements either in the mail or online. Your statements will show you the account's activity as well as how the account is progressing.

How the Stock Market Came to Be

The very first known "stock" sold was the Dutch East India Company founded in 1602. The company also founded the Amsterdam stock exchange, where shares of the company were bought and sold by the public. The founders of the company believed that they could sell shares of their company to the public in order to get more money to do the things they wanted in the hopes that they could grow the company faster and bigger than they could alone. They were the very first company to come up with such an idea, and guess what? It worked! When the company earned a profit, it would serve to increase the value of the shares held by the public. Though today our stock exchanges are much more sophisticated, the original purpose of the exchange remains the same: sell shares to the public in order to raise money to build a bigger and better company.

Just as the Amsterdam exchange allowed the Dutch East India Company to grow and succeed, today's stock exchanges provide a way for investors and companies to share the profit (and risks) of new endeavors, such as trying to invent a cure for cancer, innovating the latest technology, or developing the latest and greatest fad. In the years since, the stock market has allowed companies of all different sizes and industry to succeed, and for investors to share in that success. The research process we discussed is imperative to determine if you should invest in a company. The process should help weed out companies that are too risky due to their market competition or their leadership.

Stock Market Basics

How does a company sell its stock on a stock exchange?

A public corporation is one that issues stock that the general public can buy and trade on stock market exchanges. Rather than stocks held by those in the company, these public stocks are owned by shareholders who are part of the general public. A company needs to have an *initial public offering* (IPO). This is traditionally done through big investment banks that help advise companies on the potential value of their company, and the market for their stock. Once the company holds their IPO, the stocks are listed on the exchange and available to the public to purchase.

Why does a company "go public"?

A company goes public because it believes that listing on a stock market gives it access to more money through the general public and investors generally. With more money, the company can make investments into new products and markets and realize its company goals, potentially faster than it could alone.

What impacts a stock's price?

What a company does and how they manage the business and communicate with the public will have a positive or negative effect on the stock price. There are also external factors that impact the stock's price, things like government regulations, changes in the general economy, competition, negative tweets from celebrities or the general public, and changes in technology. When investors think negatively of a company, they will often begin to sell the stock, which can cause the stock price to fall. Positive news can have the same effect on the upside price of the stock. The risk involved in investing is that even a well-run company can have a bad stock price due to forces beyond its control.

Investing is an ongoing process of constant review and evaluation. You cannot simply "set it and forget it." Too many things can change with the companies you bought, which can impact both stock prices and therefore your account's value and ability to achieve your goals. At least annually, make sure you review account statements with your child. Next we'll explore what these statements mean.

Reading Your Investment Account Statements

Once your child has an investment account, it's necessary for them to learn how to read their account statements. Whether you manage the investments yourself or have management outsourced to a financial advisor, it's still important that you learn to read and evaluate your account statements. Below are a few investing terms you and your children should understand and review on their statements regularly:

Cost basis: The purchase price of the investment you bought. The value is used to determine your gain or loss when you sell the investment.

Capital gains/losses: A capital gain is the profit earned on the sale of an investment. A capital loss is the loss from the sale of an investment. This is the difference between the investments cost basis and the sale price.

Return on investment (ROI): Measures the percentage gain or loss generated on an investment, compared to the amount of money you invested. Here's an example of how to evaluate your ROI:

Sally Saver bought 1 share of PIG.inc on January 10, 2010 for $10.
On February 22, 2018 she sold her share of PIG.inc for $22.
Sally's **cost basis** is $10.
Sally's **capital gain/loss** is $22 – $10 = $12.
Sally's **return on investment** is her gain/cost basis: $12/$10 = 120% ROI.

Asset allocation: A summary of how your investments are divided among different categories like stocks and bonds or other types of asset classes like US and international investments. Sally's PIG.inc was a US stock (and her only investment) so her allocation would be 100% US stocks. Asset allocation is usually illustrated on account statements as a pie chart, with each slice representing a different investment type.

Total contributions/total withdrawals: Review of the inflow and outflow of money in your accounts, the amount you put into the account, and the amount that has been taken out. The inflows will show things like money you deposited and money earned from your investments. Outflows include things like fees, trading costs, etc. Keeping an eye on these fees is critical for sustainable growth.

Fees: There are several different types of fees that may appear on your account statements. Each will be preceded with a negative (–) symbol. If you are unclear what any of the fees represent, call the number on your statement and ask. Fees can eat into your ROI over time so it's important to monitor them closely.

So far, we have focused only on stock investments, because for children stocks can be easier to understand than other types of investments. Yet there are so many different types of investments and layers within each type of investment. Here are a few other common types of investments that you can introduce to your child to help increase their financial IQ.

Bonds (or fixed income): Essentially an IOU, a bond is like a loan to the bond issuer (the government or a company) that gets paid back with interest. Bonds are expected to be relatively stable and a good alternative during times of stock market ups and downs. Both the government and corporations issue bonds to raise money. Because little risk is associated with most bonds, their return is generally lower than that of stocks and they tend to offer a bit of safety. Be advised that no all bonds offer the same levels of risk. Bonds are rated AAA through C, AAA being the highest quality and "safest" while C being the riskiest.

Mutual funds: Think of a mutual fund like owning something from multiple vendors in the farmers' market. Mutual funds are professionally managed portfolios or groups of stocks, bonds, and/or other types of investments. Instead of owning individual companies, owning one mutual fund can expose you to hundreds of companies, provide diversification, and reduce risk and your need to research each individual company. Mutual funds can also provide access to hundreds of company names for a much lower price that it would cost to buy each company individually and are great investment vehicles for those just starting out.

ETFs (exchange-traded funds): Like mutual funds, ETFs enable investors to buy and sell a portfolio of stocks, bonds, and/or other types of investments to diversify their portfolio in a low-cost way. ETFs typically also offer lower fees than mutual funds. Unlike mutual funds, ETFs trade on exchanges like stocks.

There are many types of investments that can go into an investment portfolio; these are just a few of the most common. Bonds, mutual funds, and ETFs can also be bought and sold through and advisor or an online investment account. Encourage your children to research and compare different types of investments to determine the right fit for their needs.

What type of account should you open to house your investments? I like to call the type of account you use your "tax-house." Each type of account brings with its specific tax advantages or disadvantages. For simplicity we will focus on the following three types:

1. **Taxable accounts:** The first account your child opens will be a simple investment account, one I refer to as a taxable account. A taxable account can be opened in your child's name or held jointly with a parent or a Trust account. Any profits made in the form of dividends or interest will be taxable to the account holder. Additionally, when you sell investments at a gain, the profit or gain will be taxed.

2. **Tax-deferred accounts:** In order to open a tax-deferred investment account, you must have earned income (a paying job), so your children most likely won't be exposed to tax-deferred accounts until they get their first job. Tax-deferred accounts are typically referred to as retirement accounts, essential savings and investment vehicles that help our children (and young adults) plan secure futures. Most often, companies offering their employees tax-deferred accounts, such as 401(k) plans, will match contributions that you or your children make providing "free money" which helps them save more. You pay taxes on the profits and the growth of the account only when you withdraw the money. Examples include 401(k), IRA, 403(b), etc. The laws today provide for penalty free withdrawals after age 59 1/2 or a 10% penalty on withdrawals prior to age 59 1/2; however there are some exceptions.

3. **Tax-free accounts:** Though not completely "tax-free," meaning you have already paid income tax on the money you put into these accounts, you never

pay taxes again on the dollars. Not only does the money in tax-free accounts *grow* tax free, but distributions from these types of accounts are also tax-free (subject to a few nuances). Examples include ROTH IRA and 529 accounts. ROTH IRAs are primarily used for retirement while 529 accounts are used for education.

For younger children who don't have earned income from a job and are just starting out, opening a taxable brokerage account is the first step. Once they begin to earn income from a summer job or the like, they will be eligible to invest in an IRA or ROTH IRA. Because of the tax-free benefits of the ROTH IRA, this is always my preference. This type of account is intended for long-term savings. Like most other tax-qualified accounts, with a few exceptions, money taken out before 59½ will incur a 10% penalty.

There are a few additional investing concepts that can have a major impact on growing or devaluing your investment portfolio. Two of the most important to understand are compounding and inflation:

Power of compounding: One of the ways you will be rewarded by investing regularly and for the long term is through the power of compounding returns. As Benjamin Franklin astutely said, "Money makes money. And the money that money makes, makes money."

The power of compounding is the snowball effect that happens when your earnings generate more earnings. When investors put money into their accounts on a regular basis, the interest or growth on their investments gets reinvested and continues to grow. This reinvestment of the interest creates a snowball effect which continues to build a bigger and bigger base for more growth to be generated. Visualize a snowball at the top of a long, steep hill. As the original snowball rolls down the hill, it collects more and more snow with each turn. At the end of the hill, the snowball has significantly increased in size. This is the power of compounding and the same will happen with interest on your investment portfolio.

The curved line in the figure shown here shows the power of compounding on an initial investment of $10,000, whose earnings continue to be reinvested. If you were to keep reinvesting your earnings (assuming a steady, hypothetical return of 6% each year), after 20 years your investment will have grown by $20,627. And if you've got an even longer time frame—for example, if you're in your twenties and saving for retirement—after 40 years your investment will have grown by $92,857! Compare that to *not* reinvesting: in 20 years and 40 years you will still have $10,000. Compounding returns are necessary to build wealth.

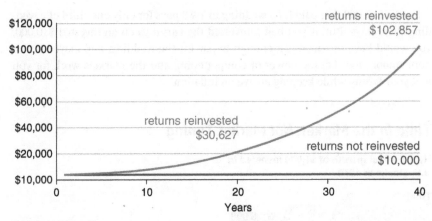

(*Source:* Vanguard.)

If you also added $100 per month, or $1,200 a year, into the $10,000 portfolio you would have more money working for you. At the end of a 40 year period you will have added $48,000 to your original $10,000 and your ending portfolio value would be $288,571! That is the power of compounding interest.

The Rule of 72 is also a great shortcut to illustrate and calculate the power of compounding. A simple go-to calculation is that if your money earns an average of 10% per year, it will take seven years to double. This rule can be a quick way to determine if you have saved enough toward your goals.

Inflation: Inflation is the increase in the overall prices of products and services in the economy. Each dollar buys less over time, and we all probably start to feel poorer as this happens. Things get more expensive with time.

When you think back on what you used to be able to buy for a dollar versus what you can get now, you get a glimpse of inflation. In the example of compounding interest above, if the investor did not reinvest their returns to get the benefit of the power of compounding, they might assume they did not lose any money. But actually the impact of inflation may have caused them to lose spending power of that money. Compare the costs of the items in the table shown here for 1988 to their costs in 2018 (*Source:* The Motley Fool):

Item	1988	2018
Milk	$2.19	$2.89
Wedding	$10,379	$33,391
The New Yorker magazine	$1.75	$8.99
Eggs per dozen	$0.71	$1.63
A first-class stamp	$0.25	$0.50

So, the $10,000 that paid for a wedding in 1988 pays for only one-third of a wedding these days. But, if you had reinvested the earnings on an invested $10,000, you would have provided just enough to pay for the wedding, and maybe a nice honeymoon, too! Let the power of compounding and the markets work for you and your family while keeping an eye on inflation.

Time *In* the Market, *Not* Market Timing

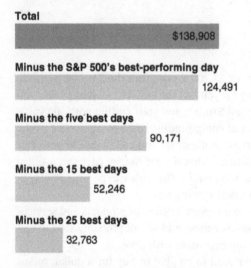

Hypothetical growth of $1,000 invested in
U.S. stocks in 1970

Total

$138,908

Minus the S&P 500's best-performing day

124,491

Minus the five best days

90,171

Minus the 15 best days

52,246

Minus the 25 best days

32,763

Note: Based on the total return of the S&P 500 from
Jan. 1, 1970, to Aug. 31, 2019

The Planning Process

The above steps will help to introduce your children and new investors to the basics. As your children grow and their needs change, they will need to layer in additional concepts that encompass a more holistic planning approach to investing.

One of my favorite tips about investing, and in fact my business tagline, is "Investing starts with a plan." I stress this because investing for the sake of investing—unless you are independently wealthy with lots of money you can afford to lose—is not a good strategy. What is a good strategy is understanding your own personal *why*. Your *why* is your dream, purpose, cause, or belief that drives you. It's critical to determine why you have investment goals and what they will cost, and to invest only after you've defined your *why*—consciously and with purpose in order to achieve those goals.

While many people think of investing as simply picking the best stocks with the highest potential return (think of my Worldcom.com and Pets.com blunder), the process of investing wisely involves many layers to selecting the right investments to meet your unique needs.

Planning in its simplest form is like the goal-setting we examined in our earlier discussion of goals: WHW: Why? How? What?

Why Am I Investing?

Is there a specific goal you are trying to achieve? Is there a specific thing you are seeking to buy or spend your investment earnings on? Just like with goal-setting, it is important to be as specific as possible. Many adults' primary goal is retirement. This is simply too broad. When do you plan to retire? How much money will you need in retirement? Investing and goal planning is something that has a long-term focus, and most children aren't ready for this until they, too, are adults and doing adult things like buying a car or purchasing their first home. Not to worry, though: if your child doesn't have their own account but you have a 529, trust, or other type of college savings account for your child, you can use those accounts to walk through the planning and investment process. Using a 529 or other type of educational savings account is a great way to explain the process. The account type defines your *why*, which in this case is college. You have a clearly defined goal and specific time when the goal will need to be met: 18 years. The next step is to determine the *how*: How much will I need, and how much risk will I take?

How Much Do I Need to Invest?

Here we need to start with the end in mind and work backwards. We have a finite amount of time to save for a goal and a finite set of resources. Using the college example, I encourage parents to consider how much they are willing to give their children for college and graduate school. Let's say you would like to give your child $100,000 toward their post-secondary education. You will need to back into how much money you need to invest each year in order to reach $100,000. A simple calculation would be to say I need $100,000 and I have 18 years to save. Divide $100,000 by 18 and you need to save $5,555.55 a year or $462.96 a month, for 18 years. If you have more than one child, you would double, triple, or quadruple that number. Fortunately our friend, compounding interest, is on our side. Bankrate.com has a great online calculator that can help you determine how much you need to save to reach a specific goal if your money is invested. You simply enter your savings goal of $100,000, enter the amount of time you must save, here 18 years, and an expected rate of return, conservatively we will use 5%. By investing and earning a return of 5%, you will need to save $285.66 a month or $3,427.92 a year to reach the $100,000 goal. Said differently, you need to invest just *$61,702.56 in order to reach your $100,000 goal.* By investing, you earned almost $40,000 toward your goal. The money you invest is making money and working for you and your goal.

How Much Risk Should I Take?

The answer to this question is personal and will be different depending on your goals. We often talk in the financial industry about risk tolerance, that is, how comfortable you are with varying levels of ups and downs in your portfolio. A typical question in determining risk tolerance is, "What would you do if your portfolio lost 25%?" If your answer is "sell everything," then you would typically be considered a conservative investor. If your response is "buy more," we would typically consider you a more aggressive investor. When we discuss balancing risk and reward, we typically try to balance taking on more risk to meet long-term goals and less risk to meet short-term goals. It's critical to align your risk levels with the amount of time you must reach your goals (known as your time horizon), and resources.

In the college example, you have 18 years to save; this is considered long term. In the early savings years, you would most likely take on more risk in the account and then as your money grows and compounds like the snowball, you may consider taking on less risk. In fact, many 529 plans have what they call "age-based" investments, where they, by design, reduce the portfolio risk every five or so years in order to capture and preserve growth. The portfolio allocation is adjusted in order to minimize the risk, usually by selling some of the stocks and replacing them with bonds.

In our example I used 18 years for savings; the reality is that you have 22 years to save for college. The 4 years your children are in school are also prime savings years.

What Should I Invest In?

Or said differently, what should my asset allocation be? Asset allocation refers to how you "combine" or "diversify" your investments, or assets. Diversifying your assets means not putting all your eggs in one basket, but rather spreading your money across US companies, bonds, real estate, international markets, and so forth, to reduce the risk in your portfolio and gain more steady returns over time. Risk should be spread across different asset classes, or types of investments, in order to collectively spread the risk and achieve the intended goal.

Because we simply don't know what types of investments will do well in the future, holding different types of investments will help you to capture gains when they do occur and help balance your risk by not having all your eggs in one basket when portions of your portfolio fall.

In our college savings example, we have properly dealt with the *why* and the *how* so that the *what* is relatively easy. Our plan includes a post-secondary education goal of $100,000 with a time horizon of 18 years and with an aggressive risk profile. As I mentioned earlier if you are saving in a 529 plan, they make the asset allocation selection easy for you. Most other online investment platforms offer similar guidance. You can either select a mutual fund that has a risk identified with yours (e.g. aggressive) or most platforms also have what are called model portfolios. These portfolios are constructed with a set of investments stocks, bonds, mutual funds, ETFs, and so on, each working together to create an expected risk and return. Here, an aggressive portfolio would be designed with very little or no bonds with the expectation that it will perform better than a more moderate or conservative type of investment.

Your children should revisit their *why, how,* and *what* annually. Have your goals changed? Life has a way of throwing us curve balls and turning our world upside down. Perhaps something has come up that caused you to save less for a certain period of time. Go back and revisit your *why, how,* and *what,* and then make the appropriate adjustments.

Finally, the stock market can be volatile and provide unexpected returns. Viewing your accounts' total performance and understanding if you need to take more or less risk in the portfolio is a critical step in the annual evaluation.

Each year ask yourself: Am I still on track to meet my goals? If not, what needs to change?

Next we look at the psychology of investing and how you and your child's behavior can affect the growth of your investments and the success of your plan.

The Psychology of Investing

Believe it or not, market returns have more to do with human behavior than investment skill. Fortunately, if children get introduced to the concepts and emotional impact of investing at a young age, they will have a greater chance to master both money management and management of their own behavior surrounding money. Money has a huge influence on human behavior and understanding why we make certain decisions about money can help us to avoid making poor financial and investment decisions.

Lori Santos, a cognitive psychologist, studies primate psychology and "monkeynomics," testing problems in human psychology on primates, which have many of the same predictable irrationalities as humans. Santos set out to learn why a species as evolved as humans continues to repeat the same mistakes even when presented with negative data to the contrary. She started her study by teaching monkeys how to use money.

She designed a special "monkey marketplace," a separate cage accessible from the normal monkey living space, complete with open slots that enabled the animals to interact with experimenters and go shopping. She gave the monkeys "wallets" filled with small, coin-like tokens, and had two experimenters pose as marketplace vendors, offering food through the slots in exchange for tokens.

The monkeys quickly mastered the rules of basic exchange. They learned to deposit a token into the outstretched hand of a trader and receive the piece of food being offered by the other hand. They even learned to recognize a sale, purchasing more apples when the price dropped. The next experiment presented the monkeys with two options. The first was to spend a token on one piece of food that half the time would change to two pieces of food or to spend the token on two pieces of food that half of the time would change to one piece of food. Reason would tell us that the monkeys should not care how they spend their tokens because the odds are 50–50 that they get one or two pieces in either scenario. In Santos's experiment, the monkeys vastly preferred the first option. They preferred a 50–50 chance at a gain instead of a 50–50 chance at a loss.

What Santos learned from the monkeynomics experiment is that the monkeys displayed natural biases, like those we see in humans when they invest. Specifically, the monkeys exhibited a bias known as loss aversion. They worked harder to avoid losing money than they did to gain it. She concluded that our natural biases are hard to overcome because they are part of our biological limitations. Many say we are hardwired this way. She reasoned that even though monkeys and humans share the same biases, because humans are a more evolved species, we possess the ability to identify and recognize our limitations and therefore can overcome them.

When investing, overcoming our own negative behaviors and emotions in order to stay the course of our investment plans can be one of our most difficult challenges. The world of behavioral finance defines our natural biases as a series of *cognitive biases*, or mistakes in reasoning, evaluating, or remembering that are often the result of holding onto our beliefs regardless of contrary information. Like the monkeys, who worked harder at avoiding losses, these cognitive biases often trick investors and result in decision making that negatively impacts investment returns and the realization of goals.

Loss aversion when investing is the idea that investors are more sensitive to investment losses than they are to gains. In fact, investors feel the pain of losses twice as much as they feel the pleasure of gains. This phenomenon often causes investors to overreact to investment losses, and sometimes causes them to sell at market bottoms, missing out on future gains. This is also known as selling low instead of buying low. Unfortunately, we saw a good deal of this type of behavior during the period of 2008–2009.

Just as it is important to understand your money personality, it is critical to understand your personal biases as they may cause you to deviate from your investment plan. For example, you may develop a reliance on "noise," or information from the media or friends that could cause you to react by buying or selling at the exact wrong time. Watch how your children react during their first investment experience and see if you notice any of the following biases. If you can identify their biases, you can help them to think through their concerns and even identify their own biases to make them more mindful of their behavior.

A few other types of biases include:

Recency bias: The tendency to overvalue more recent information.
Bandwagon bias: The tendency to want to conform to be part of a crowd.
Status-quo bias: The tendency to resist change even when it may be financially beneficial to change.
Anchoring: The tendency to anchor on the first piece of information you receive when making decisions and not consider any other information.
Confirmation bias: The tendency to search out information that validates your viewpoint.

Mindful investing means becoming aware of our natural behaviors and biases about investing in order to not repeat mistakes. Remember, investing is not only the study of finance, it is the study of how people behave with money. Teach your children to have a process and then control what they can.

Things you cannot control include:

- Inflation
- Returns
- Market

Things you can control include:

- Costs
- How much risk you take
- Asset allocation
- *Your* own behavior

All these concepts can be built upon as your child's investments and needs grow. Luckily there is no shortage of wonderful books that teach investing concepts to all ages and I've included a list of my favorites in Chapter 15.

Insurance

The word *insurance* can be traced back to the Latin work *securus* or "free from care." Keep this in mind when you discuss insurance with your children. Insurance is essentially a payment made to company for security against a financial loss or damage. Auto insurance is a payment made to protect one from a financial loss from an auto accident. Health insurance is a payment made to protect one from a financial loss due to an illness or health issue. Though there are a few types of insurance I believe everyone should have, and perhaps others as one's level of assets increases, each one meant to protect a person from financial loss, unfortunately, there are many policies that are structured in unnecessarily complicated ways. Below are the policies I believe everyone should have and the information you should know about these policies. If you can't understand the policy, you or your child should not own it.

For each of the four types of insurance listed below, make sure you and your children are clear and can articulate the following:

Deductible = The amount you must pay before the insurance company will begin to pay on a claim.

Coverage = Understand what exactly is included *and* what is excluded. Keep in mind where you live, nature of the asset you are covering, and the potential risks.

Premium = Cost you pay for coverage.

How to process a claim = Whom to call or contact when you need to execute on a policy.

I also suggest keeping notes or a summary of the above for each policy or have your financial advisor do it for you. I find that though you may understand the coverage when buying the policy, when you need the policy your recollection may be fuzzy. Notes will help you know exactly what to do and what to expect from your insurance policy.

1. **Auto insurance.** Most states require the bare minimum of liability coverage. There are other things to consider, like the age of your car, the value of your car, and your monthly cashflow as well, as if you lease or have a loan on your vehicle, the bank may require a certain level of coverage.

2. **Homeowners' insurance.** Homeowners' insurance is meant to protect you from a financial loss if damage occurs to your home. Since your home will

likely be your child's biggest asset for a good portion of their life, insuring it is crucial. Your coverage will depend on the cost of your home, its location, and location will also dictate other types of home insurance protection such as flood and earthquake. The most basic is appropriately called basic coverage while the next level is considered a broad form of coverage and typically will include not only your housing structure, but also items inside the home. Keep in mind if something isn't listed as covered, it is not. In South Carolina we have hurricanes that cause significant damage and it is often only after the fact that many people try to submit a claim only to learn than their policy does not include any damage to the home from the wind. We were also new to having to buy a termite bond on a home. Without one your entire home could be lost to those pesky bugs and you would have to pay to fix it completely out of pocket, another reason to investigate what specific coverage is needed for your unique situation. If you rent and do not own a home, renters' insurance should be purchased in order to protect your valuables.

3. **Health insurance.** This really should be listed first. You are your biggest asset! Most companies will offer your children insurance when they get their first job; it will be an expense, but it is a must. Depending on the company's size and offerings it could be less than $100 to a few hundred a month and will increase as the size of their family increases. There has been a significant increase in what is called 1099 employment versus W-2 employment. W-2 employees are given all of the benefits a firm offers while 1099 employees are considered independent and must find their own health insurance. We have the "open market," which has made some healthcare more accessible to those not covered by a work plan. There are also lots of healthcare agents who can help your child get the best policy and coverage needed.

4. **Life insurance.** There are so many versions of this it will make your head spin. At its most basic, life insurance is bought for income replacement. What if you suffer a premature death? How much money would be needed to cover and settle all of your debts and provide for your loved ones? As your family grows, this figure will get larger. A policy called "term" life insurance is for a specific term or number of years. For instance, when viewing the policy as an income replacement, most people will buy a term policy up through their working years. So if you expect to work another 30 years, the term should be 30 years. The longer the policy and the younger you are when you get the policy, the lower the premiums annually. At the end of the term, the coverage is gone and so, too, are any benefits. Another type of policy is called a "whole life" policy. Contrast the term policy with a whole life, which is considered a "permanent" policy. A whole life policy is more of an investment. Here you are paying an annual premium for some future benefit that gets paid when you die. The cost of the whole life policy is more expensive than a term simply

because we all die, so while insurance companies don't know when, they know for sure they will have to pay the death benefit. Often people use this so they know there is a specific amount they are leaving to their loved ones, or to pay the cost of estate taxes or to fund a trust for their children upon their death. Each requires a physical exam in order for the insurance companies to under-write or offer the policy. The healthier you are, the better rating you get and the less expensive your premiums will be.

In addition to the information above, for life insurance policies you should also make note and understand the following:

Death benefit = The amount the insurance company will pay your beneficiaries when you die.

Beneficiaries = You list both primary and contingent. If the primary named ben-eficiaries are dead, the money passes to the contingent. Those named will receive the death benefit amount.

Cash value = In a whole life policy, your payments over the years may create a cash bucket. This cash bucket is filled up from part of the premium you pay on insurance. In some cases the bucket gets filled up enough to cover your pre-mium payments for a period of time.

When considering insurance, hire a reputable company, one that has been in business for a very long time. Proper insurance can protect you and your family from financial catastrophe.

Again, there are endless opportunities to talk to and teach your kids about investing. Here are some actionable steps to get the ball rolling at different ages:

Elementary: Before you can invest regularly, you need to have regular income. Now is the time for kids to explore their first income-making ventures. (Think lemonade stand.)

Tweens: Make your child a part of the financial planning and investment process in your home. If you have a college savings account, show them how the account is invested, or have them sit with your financial advisor to explain how it works. Most financial advisors are willing to sit and share knowledge with young adults. Show them simple stock market charts. Find an app to help them understand markets and start tracking a stock or two.

Teens: Particularly in middle school, children may get part-time summer jobs or work in family businesses to help out. Jacob has been working in my office since he was nine, stuffing envelopes, shredding paper, updating spreadsheets, organizing files. There are lots of things kids can do to earn money.

Use bank savings to open an investment account to invest in a stock or two. Once your kids have earned income, they can open a ROTH account. ROTH accounts are my favorite. Money is invested and grows tax free, forever! The money can be used prior to retirement (age 59½) for a limited number of things, including first home purchases. If your children have earned money and can take a portion to save and invest in a ROTH, this is a great time to do it. They can simply purchase a mutual fund or few stocks they like. They can track their investments on their phone or when statements come in.

College & Beyond: Encourage your kids to read, consume, and learn as much about investing as they can. Insist they participate in company 401(k) programs available to them and put away as much money as they can. The earlier they start investing, the sooner they'll reach their financial goals.

While investing dollars is important, it's just as important for young adults to invest in themselves. Often when financially successful people are asked "What was your best investment?" they do not say anything about the stock market, their portfolio, or income. Instead, their answers tend to be more personal, about schooling, or family, or reading. There are so many different forms of capital that drive our success; financial capital is just one ingredient. What I find helpful is to reinforce the idea that money is just a tool. It is not the goal. Money alone can buy freedom, but it can't make us happy. It's important for young adults to explore what will make them as individuals happy in their own lives.

Money-Minded Motivation

- ✓ Investing should not be a short-term game, but rather a long-term journey.
- ✓ Investing is necessary to building wealth.
- ✓ Introduce your children to investing; once their savings bucket is full, have them research and find stocks to buy.
- ✓ Small investments at a young age will reduce intimidation and will teach the basics of risk and reward to your child.
- ✓ At least annually, review your account statements with your child.
- ✓ Discuss protecting your most precious assets with the proper insurance.

11

The Bucket Approach: Putting It All Together

As our children get older they move away from the piggybank and Moonjar and into the intangible world of bank accounts—a world that seems somewhat ethereal or otherworldly. Our money comes out of our hands and *poof!* is now somewhere else that we can't touch or see except on a piece of paper we receive once a month. Now, it is in fact *somewhere*, and if you are banking with a credible institution, is safe, but it certainly is a shift from seeing how much money you have in your hands to looking at an online bank statement or using a piece of plastic to get and spend those dollars. We take this for granted and have learned to accept this as the normal course of things. However, what many of us lose in this process is the discipline of separating our saving, spending, and sharing, because now all of our money is comingled. We no longer have our money in separate jars, each tagged to a particular purpose; now everything is in one big lump sum. Why haven't we carried those lessons from our physical piggybank into our virtual piggybanks—ease, simplicity, bank fees, and so on? It is time to go back to basics and mimic this bucket approach in the virtual world of banking.

I have seen more than my share of adults struggle with managing credit cards, debit cards, bank accounts, and the like. Additionally, I took for granted that my son Jacob would completely get the idea of the debit card. He has had a savings account for several years, as well as a small ROTH IRA account. He looks at the statements and can generally read them and understand that they are for his future, his savings—in other words, this isn't money to be spent. When he was 13 we took his Moonjar money along with a couple of birthday checks and deposited them into a brand-new checking account. We sat with the bank teller and he set up his online banking passwords, pin, and so forth. I was feeling proud and happy that he was well on his way to financial wellness, in fact, that he was ahead of the game.

Prior to this, he was keeping his money in the back of his phone or in his school or gym backpack. He never really had a pulse on how much money he had to spend at any given time because it was all over the place. Now, I love the idea of a wallet, but my husband doesn't carry one and Jacob never picked up the habit and so his spending money was essentially in pockets and backpacks, if it wasn't in the Moonjar bank. I thought the debit card would solve so many issues; he could look online and always see his balance, he could find one place to keep his card, and life would be simple and good. Where I missed the boat, completely, is that I really didn't explain how a debit card works. I took for granted that he would know and understand that this bank account is now different from other accounts that he has designated for savings. He was used to the idea that money in his hand or backpack was his to spend while the other money he really couldn't see was his to save. The debit card was just a piece of plastic and did not, for him, represent spending money. I did not anticipate this lack of awareness and understanding; in hindsight, many of us earn first, then save, spend, and share. Here, he wasn't truly earning his spending money; most of it was being given to him. Though he understood the individual concepts, putting them all together was a bit more complex.

Here is the simple bucket approach I used to tie everything together. I hope you find it useful for your children as well.

Buckets

Imagine each of the images shown here as a bucket; each bucket has a maximum capacity that you assign to it. When it reaches max capacity or gets filled up, the water will flow like a waterfall into the next bucket until full.

As your children get older, this process should be reevaluated. As their level of income increases, so will the complexity of the buckets. When earnings come in regularly, the Save will increase and be more than enough to cover the short-term goals. When your child is working and earning a real paycheck, not from the bank of Mom and Dad, the Save bucket begins to expand but can only hold so much water. A short-term goal bucket begins to overflow into the Invest buckets of 401(k), ROTH IRA, and/or investment accounts. Invest buckets are used to fund longer term goals we call the freedom fund.

The importance of this lesson is for your child to have a process, a plan, and a purpose for their money. I have recently learned about the Reality Check program run by Yukon Public School District in Yukon, Oklahoma. This is a one-day event for the freshman class of students. All students are required to attend. Each student is given their "adult identity" in which they are assigned a career, salary, and some a spouse and others between one and three children

Account 1	Account 2	Account 3
Save	Share	Spend
30%	**20%**	**50%**
Fill up the SAVE bucket first—commit to 30%; this will create a strong foundation for your children to save 30% of what they earn for their future self. Learning this habit at a young age will create an automatic response to place all future earnings into the savings bucket.	The next bucket is SHARE, which can range anywhere from 0 to 30% depending on your and your children's preference. Here we will say 20%. This may be high, depending on your children's level of earnings and can certainly be adjusted or modified. The purpose here is just to create the habit of designating a sharing bucket	The last bucket is SPEND. Seeing that we can only spend what is left over will create the habit of budgeting. The balance of 50% will flow into the SPEND bucket. This is how much your children have to spend at any particular time. When the money begins to run low, they will need to learn the skill of how to *earn*.
Short-Term Goals	Charitable Donations	Entertainment
Emergency Funds	Gift Giving	Eating Out

Credit: Artist Tami Boyce

Once given their identity they are released into the school cafeteria into the mock community of businessmen and businesswomen. Each table represents a different business or way to spend their paycheck. The booths signify real-life spending like clothing, groceries, doctors, phone, day care, credit cards, and cars, as well as savings 401(k), ROTH IRA, healthcare, and student loans.

Along with their adult identity the freshman are sent to the "Uncle Sam" booth to collect their student card, which lists their monthly income, net of taxes and Social Security and Medicare payments. Next they are free to save, spend, and share at their own will. Each booth is led by a community volunteer, in which they discuss their spending options and then make a selection of what to purchase or how much to spend. The kids have complete autonomy to use the money as they wish.

Once they travel through their monthly paycheck all spending is calculated for them. The total shows the reality of their spending and, as you've probably guessed, most spend more than they make. It's a great way for kids to learn how to budget and then bring these lessons back into the classroom to analyze why and where each person overspent and develop better habits so that when they do enter the real world, this lesson of going into debt or bouncing checks due to overspending is already behind them.

This is the type of creativity we need to bring more of to our children. Finding new and unique ways for our kids to practice personal finance is a great source of learning than can help influence our kids' personal wealth journey.

A Note About Our Girls

Every year in March we celebrate International Women's Day (March 8). It's a global celebration of the social, economic, cultural, and political achievements of women. Women in the United States and other developed countries have much more to celebrate than many women in emerging and frontier countries who still struggle immensely. But one thing is sure: women have come a long way over the past century.

In April, we celebrate financial literacy month. Even with the great strides women have made, this is an area where we still have a long way to go. As a financial advisor, there are two statistics that plague me daily and give me great concern for many women. The first is that, according to the US Census Bureau, 80% of women will outlive their husbands, many by more than 14 years. The second, according to the Institute of Divorce Financial Analysts, is that women who get divorced typically live at 45% of their pre-divorce lifestyle.

Let's start with the first statistic: women will outlive men, yet most women will earn less and save less than their spouses over their lifetimes. There are many reasons for this. Some women may choose to take time out of the workforce to care for children, decreasing pension and Social Security dollars. Even those who remain in the workforce earn on average 80 cents compared to every $1 a man makes. Retirement savings is a struggle for most people, but the odds are stacked against women. Even more troubling is that many women are in the dark about their financial resources and liabilities. Every couple manages their financial house differently. Some spouses take more financial ownership than others and, like any household chore, it's often divide-and-conquer just to keep up with life. However, this doesn't excuse ignorance in financial matters. More often than I would like to admit, I speak to women who have recently lost their spouse and are not only grieving but are completely blind to their financial assets, liabilities, and general income needs to run their household.

The second statistic regarding divorce—that women who get divorced live at 45% of their pre-divorce lifestyle—has a similar cause. The average duration of a marriage that ends in divorce is eight years. For many marriages eight years in, there are children involved, and often the wife in a traditional marriage takes time off to focus on the children. Time out of the workforce and sleep deprivation as a new parent often put a strain on the ability to focus on much else, which leads many women to defer financial management of the household to their husbands. This can often leave the wife again in the dark about financial matters. In the event of divorce, which is now hovering around 50%, women often get the short end of the bargaining stick because they are simply without knowledge of their financial situation.

The Girl Scouts Research Institute found only 12% of girls feel confident making personal financial decisions. Every person should feel financially empowered. Fortunately, as with most things in life, proper planning can help to prepare women financially, for whatever the future may bring for them. This means helping our girls get an early start on understanding financial matters and becoming financially well, independently. Engaging our girls in financial matters will help them to become financially independent and able in their adult years. For our girls, being and staying informed has never been more important.

In addition to helping girls feel more confident making financial decisions, I want to see more girls in financial careers. I have worked in the financial services profession since day 1 out of undergraduate school. When I entered the profession it was 95% male, and the few females working as financial advisors were considered "hard" and "cold." This is certainly not true of all, but I am just sharing my experience. There were so few women that often women saw other women as competition for the very few positions we could hold. Or women were in a support or administrative role. The business of providing advice was very different then. It was purely and completely a sales profession. Stocks were bought and sold, commissions were earned, fees were excessive, and there was very little if any planning work going on. Today, I firmly believe our industry is ripe for females. However, I continue to be disheartened when I speak to young adults and ask them who in the group is considering a profession in finance. I still see the male hands outnumber the female hands by a large majority.

Consider this for your daughters: a profession that helps people; a profession that helps people define, plan, and accomplish their unique purpose; a

(Continued)

A Note About Our Girls   (Continued)

profession that aligns people's personal and financial resources with their goals, celebrates their wins, and empathizes with their losses. That is what a good financial advisor does for her clients. There continues to be a prevalent belief about finances, personal financial management, and careers in finance that it's a profession for men and that men are better suited to the profession and personal aspects of finance than women. *This is simply false.* Let's teach our girls that personal and professional finance is exactly where they need to be. The world needs more people who really listen and provide unique solutions to others to help them become financially well. If you see a spark in your girl, let that light burn bright!

12

What Does a Good Financial Advisor Do?

There will most likely be a time in your life or your child's life when your financial needs become complex and you find that you don't have the time or interest to learn to manage all the components of managing your money. Investing, college costs, retirement, tax implications—it can all become time consuming and overwhelming. When this time comes, you need to find a *fiduciary* advisor who can help you establish a solid financial foundation and stay on track to meeting your investment goals.

Many people outsource certain aspects of their investment plan upkeep, just as many outsource certain aspects of caring for their homes. We hire professionals who have both the time and expertise to handle all the work involved. The same is true of investing. A good financial professional provides her clients with the support, tools, clarification, and guidance to meet personal, financial, and professional goals. A true financial advisor views the profession as a helping profession, a multidisciplinary field that requires foundational skills and knowledge ranging from economics to psychology to negotiation, as well as superb listening skills and empathy.

Yet hiring the right type of investment professional is important. With so many labels in the industry it is difficult to know the difference between a broker, registered representative, financial advisor, wealth advisor, registered investment advisor, and so on. There is a *fiduciary standard* that only certain types of investment professionals, no matter their title, are required to honor.

Only "registered investment advisors" (RIAs) are held by law to a fiduciary standard of care. What that means, simply, is that RIAs must put their clients' best interests ahead of their own. In practice this means that an RIA, legally, cannot sell a product to a person simply because they will earn the highest level of fee. It means that an RIA will not treat everyone who is 50 years old the same; they will take the time to walk through a discovery process in which they understand not only their clients' risk tolerance, but their goals, dreams, financial resources, and money personality. Sadly, not all financial advisors are required by law to provide advice that is in the best interest of the client, which has created a great deal of confusion and labeled our industry, one that I believe to be a remarkable helping profession, as a sales profession full of pushy people selling products that are too expensive and that most people don't understand.

Many professionals who call themselves "advisors," or "consultants," or "planners" are only legally held to what is known as a *suitability standard*, where there are minimal requirements for selling products or even different standards of care depending on the type of account. Selling products is very different from providing advice. The suitability standard only requires that the advisor sell investments they believe are "suitable" for their clients, not necessarily what is in their clients' best interest. It is an extremely and unnecessarily confusing concept to understand, and even financial industry regulators grapple with the laws every day.

In an effort to simplify the concept, I offer the following analogy:

You find yourself at the doctor's office. You have self-diagnosed and asked for a script. Dr. Suitable asks you a few questions:

How old are you?
Have you ever taken this script before?
Why do you need the script?

Doctor Suitable checks the box and writes you a script. You never see him again.

Now, Dr. Fiduciary enters the room and reviews your chart:

Tell me why you requested this medication?
Tell me about your symptoms.
I see that you are 45. How long have you been experiencing these issues?
Tell me about your family history. Do you exercise? What other medications do you take?

Doctor Fiduciary performs a full physical and determines that, though the requested medication may not harm you, you will have much better results with script Y and asks that you return annually so that she may evaluate your progress and modify the dosage as your symptoms improve.

The difference here is not the level of education of the physician, the fancy office space, or even the intellect. The difference is the *level of care* you receive.

The same holds true in the financial world. It's extremely important to ask any financial professional you consider hiring to manage your money whether they are a fiduciary. If the answer is no, understand why not and consider the impact to yourself and your long-term investment goals.

When you or your children first start their investing journey, often it will be their first ROTH account or 401(k) account through work. For smaller accounts or 401(k) accounts, they will not need to hire a financial advisor; however, what they will need is a plan. Consider gifting your child the services of a Certified Financial Planner when they get their first job. A Certified Financial Planner (CFP) can help guide your child to help them plan to save, how much to save, pay off debt, understand where and how to invest, and so much more. Preferably, your children take the advice and implement it directly with an online trading custodian, keeping costs low and automating their savings. As we discussed in the investing section there are a variety of different retail trading platforms that allow anyone to set up automatic contributions and buy into a designed portfolio or series of investments each month.

As your children begin to accumulate more assets their financial situation will become more complex. At this point they should revisit their plan with their CFP and discuss whether they need to make any changes. If this requires them to open new accounts or transfer retirement assets from an old job, either the CFP can recommend an RIA, or chances are they are an RIA who can help you with this process. Most RIAs are also CFPs, that is, they build, design, and execute life plans for their client, not just manage money. A good RIA will also act as the quarterback to help coordinate tax issues with your CPA, addressing any issues with a Will or powers of attorney, including making sure you have them in place. Most kids won't have to worry about hiring a CPA or filing taxes until their working years begin, but it is important to find someone who is willing to work with you and your other professionals as a team. This saves time and creates efficiencies, not to mention more smart people working on your behalf to help you reach your goals.

When looking for a financial advisor, make sure your children are armed with these 15 questions to ask and understand the responses to them:

1) Will you act as a fiduciary on all of my accounts?
2) Are you a registered investment advisor?
3) What type of services do you provide?
4) Are you a certified financial planner?
5) How do you charge for your services and how much?
6) Do you get paid from anyone other than me for your services?
7) Do you outsource any aspects of your business?
8) What is your investment philosophy?
9) What custodian do you use?
10) What asset allocation will you use for my family and why?
11) How will our relationship work?
12) What are your qualifications?
13) Can you tell me about your professional experience and why you chose to be a financial advisor?
14) Do you have an account asset value or fee minimum?
15) What does your typical client look like?

The answers to these questions will help you and your family make an informed decision about whether the person is right for you. I recommend that you interview more than one person and then make a decision. A good financial advisor will learn more about you than most of your close friends. It can be a vulnerable feeling, but believe me, the more they know about what you and your family really want, the better they can help you be accountable for your goals and also provide you with customized advice. I would encourage you as a parent, if you have a current financial advisor, to ask them the above questions and make sure you are satisfied with the answers. I would also ask them if they are willing to help you and your child learn to be financially well. A good one will help your child get started.

At my firm we took the time to read the wonderful book *The ONE Thing* by Gary Keller (Bard Press, 2013). It caused us to reflect and articulate what we do for our clients and how we want to continue to provide for our clients. This is what we settled on: *We inspire personal wealth; we empower you to wake up every day with a plan, knowing what you desire, where you are going, and how to get there.* The job of financial advisors is to provide you with clarity to live your purpose. It's truly a magical experience to journey with clients through the hard work and life's ups and downs, celebrating their hard work and determination when they achieve their goals and purpose. It's quite beautiful and we all deserve to have this type of partner in our financial journey. Don't settle for less. Demand more for yourself and your children.

13

Last Thoughts

As a parent you must realize that, like you, your child is the only one responsible for their personal and financial success or failure. Knowledge is power and since much of what is in this book and what our children need to be financially well is not taught in the classroom, it is up to us to impart this knowledge to our children.

We have talked a lot about being conscious, being present, and the profound changes in technology and globalization that require a perspective shift, all these things changing the way we live and work and raise our children. To put it more deliberately, as our society and economy evolve, much of our thinking and emotional responses to these changes also evolve. I distinctly recall the first time I was introduced to Maslow's Hierarchy of Needs in my Psychology 101 class. I was deeply drawn to it. In its simplest form it gave me hope that there is more to reach for; in its most complex it drew for me the reality of where we were as a nation and society compared to so many others around the world. Our lowest low is well above many countries in our global society.

For those unfamiliar with or with a fuzzy recollection of the theory, simplypsychology.org provides the following explanation and illustration:

> Maslow's hierarchy of needs is a motivational theory in psychology comprising a five-tier model of human needs, often depicted as hierarchical levels within a pyramid.

> Needs lower down in the hierarchy must be satisfied before individuals can attend to needs higher up. From the bottom of the hierarchy upwards, the needs are physiological, safety, love and belonging, esteem, and self-actualization.

I often review the diagram and wonder if the highest point of the pyramid, self-actualization, is actually a luxury held by just a very few. The evolution of our brains and specifically our reasoning has led us to climb Maslow's Hierarchy. Visually we are moving from the Esteem needs of prestige and feelings of accomplishment toward Self-actualization, achieving our full potential as humans. Of course, everyone's journey is unique; my focus is on where our society is heading and how we must learn to adapt and specifically shift our perspective on financial matters. Some call this place we are heading The Age of Transcendence. In his book, "A Whole New Mind" (Riverhead Books, 2006), Daniel Pink calls this The Conceptual Age. He does a remarkable job of explaining how the use of our ever-fascinating brain will continue to evolve ahead of or alongside the fast-paced world we occupy.

I am not sure what to call it or specifically how to define it, but I have seen and continue to see the evolution in my industry and in the way we want and need to utilize our financial resources. One of the reasons we have as a society managed to move and scale the pyramid into the next "age" in my opinion is directly related to our abundance.

Abundance creates access to things we never dreamed of and will continue to present us with more than we could ever use in one lifetime. How do we manage and control ourselves and our children when everything we desire is just a click away? As a person on the path of financial wellness, it is important to balance the things we can obtain with our financial resources with those things we can attain that will feed our souls and enrich our lives and the lives of those around us. Yes, there is a prescriptive nature to financial wellness. The saving, spending, sharing, and investing must follow a disciplined process—one that leads to accumulated financial wealth. But there is also a new element we must embrace for ourselves and our children: the *wellness* in financial wellness. Remember the definition we discussed earlier? Financial wellness is a state of wellbeing where an individual has achieved minimal financial stress, established a strong financial foundation, and created an ongoing plan to help reach future financial goals. I am going to introduce a new concept here: *personal wealth*, the kind of wealth that has little to do with your balance sheet.

Personal Wealth = The ability to leverage all your personal assets, both tangible and intangible, to create a life that fulfills your purpose.

I believe we can and must help our children obtain their unique sense of financial wellness and in turn realize true personal wealth.

Money-Minded Motivation

- ✓ It is never too early to start educating the next generation appropriately about how to be "good with money."
- ✓ Experience is the best teacher. Children should be entrusted with enough money with no strings attached to learn from personal trial and error.
- ✓ Broaden the definition of wealth to include human, intellectual, and social capital.
- ✓ Educating the next generation is hard work and it never ends.
- ✓ The payoff can be enormous, as measured by growth in all definitions of family capital.

14

Family Mission Statement

Money should be considered a tool to help you live your life's purpose.

A significant part of what we do as parents is hope, and some of us may pray, that the things we do with our kids, the lessons we share, the values we instill, the constant reminders (perhaps nagging) about right and wrong, stick. We hope they stick. We hope that when we send our children out into the big world, that the foundation we have helped to build is one that supports them throughout the rest of their life. Jacob is now 13 and honestly I thought I had more years to mold and shape and direct him. What I am learning is that at some point we shift from dictating to our kids how to act to pulling back and gently guiding and influencing. I have recently made the shift to guide and it's not easy, but I do understand that it is a necessary part of our children's development. Our kids will make horrible decisions and we must let them, not because we are bad parents but because they are simply still learning.

As we become guides, we must find ways to gently reinforce our values and the lessons we want our children to carry with them. Creating a family mission statement is a great way to instill your values as a family and serve as a constant reminder for whom you aspire to be both as a family and as individuals. I often have the privilege of working with families who have strong sense of family, of who everyone is, how they contribute to the family, and how their ancestors have provided them with guidance and honor. The sense of pride families have in who they are and where they came from often leaves me feeling a bit empty. Keep in mind, many of these families are first-generation wealth, so in most cases I am not referring to trust funds or legacies of significant wealth (of course there is some of that, but most of these families' money comes from other types of capital). To overcome that feeling of emptiness and to create what I was looking for in my own family, we created a family mission statement.

Creating a family mission statement can help guide a family to form a deeply connected bond that gives each family member a purpose and drives them to inspire and achieve personal wealth.

This is our family mission statement:

Mackara Family
We believe that our purpose as a family is to care for Each other, our community, and the world around us. We will accomplish this by prioritizing our time together, Giving to those in need, and integrating our individual and Collective passions into each other's lives. We will make Our home a place of laughter, communication, and warmth. We will take nothing for granted, we will work hard, have Fun, give generously, live for adventure, conduct ourselves With dignity and grace, listen to each other, to our Community, and to our own hearts. We will have faith in Our dreams, in each other and in God. We will interact With each other and the world around us with a spirit of Kindness, compassion, integrity, and humor. We will, together, seek adventure and wisdom.

Each family of course will have vastly different goal, purposes, beliefs, wants, and desires, and each mission statement should reflect the family's individuality. Here is an exercise that can help your family build your own.

Our Family Mission Statement:

1. What are a few (4) strengths of each member of our family?
   Dad:_____
   Mom:_____
   Child(ren):_____

2. What types of things are we able to accomplish as a family?
   _____
   _____
   _____
   _____
   _____

3. What are practical ways that we can serve each other?
   _____
   _____
   _____
   _____

4. How can we use what we have to make the world a better place?

_____
_____
_____
_____
_____

5. What are the top four priorities we want our family to value?

_____
_____
_____
_____
_____

6. What are practical ways we can serve others outside of our family?

_____
_____
_____
_____

7. What types of things are most important to us?

_____
_____
_____
_____

8. Name three things we could do better as a family?

_____
_____
_____
_____

9. If we could name one principle from which we want our family to operate, what would it be?

_____
_____
_____
_____
_____

10. What is one way we are unique as a family?

_____

_____

_____

_____

_____

Conclusion

Talking about money and family finances is not particularly easy, but instead of belaboring what to say and how to say it, simply *do it*. Remember kids learn every time you use your credit card, grab takeout, shop for gifts, go to the grocery, or online shop. Every day brings opportunity to show children and young adults about the simple process of spending, saving, and investing, and also to demonstrate the values that guide your choices. I want you and your children to live in a place where you spend and save thoughtfully, where your behaviors and thinking about your finances contribute to your personal wellbeing, and where anything is possible.

My hope is that you will begin to create a planning mindset with your family, that you will achieve minimal financial stress, establish a strong financial foundation, and create a plan to help align your values with your goals. Your money journey can be incorporated into your life journey.

Know that every action you take in relation to wealth accumulation and financial management is designed to move your life, and the life of your children, in the direction of your purpose. As you set that mindset and vision, you design *your plan* and remove your sabotage patterns to build the sound financial management practices needed to accomplish your *why*.

When we talk about being money-minded or financially well, it's not about blind ambition or being focused on and consumed with money. It is truly about creating good habits so that you and your family can live with little financial stress, manage your lives with clarity, and most importantly enjoy your lives. I will leave you with the Mexican Fisherman fable, which illustrates this concept beautifully. Use this story as inspiration to slow down, reassess, and get real about how you are living and what you are teaching your children by example.

The Mexican Fisherman

An American investment banker was at the pier of a small coastal Mexican village when a small boat with just one fisherman docked. Inside the small boat were several large yellowfin tuna. The American complimented the Mexican on the quality of his fish and asked how long it took to catch them.

The Mexican replied, "Only a little while." The American then asked why he didn't stay out longer and catch more fish. The Mexican said he had enough to support his family's immediate needs. The American then asked, "But what do you do with the rest of your time?"

The Mexican fisherman said, "I sleep late, fish a little, play with my children, take siestas with my wife, Maria, stroll into the village each evening where I sip wine, and play guitar with my amigos. I have a full and busy life." The American scoffed, "I am a Harvard MBA and could help you. You should spend more time fishing and with the proceeds, buy a bigger boat. With the proceeds from the bigger boat, you could buy several boats. Eventually you would have a fleet of fishing boats. Instead of selling your catch to a middleman, you would sell directly to the processor, eventually opening your own cannery. You would control the product, processing, and distribution. You would need to leave this small coastal fishing village and move to Mexico City, then LA, and eventually New York City, where you will run your expanding enterprise."

The Mexican fisherman asked, "But, how long will this all take?"

To which the American replied, "Fifteen to twenty years."

"But what then?" asked the Mexican.

The American laughed and said, "That's the best part. When the time is right you would announce an IPO and sell your company stock to the public and become very rich—you would make millions!"

"Millions—then what?"

The American said, "Then you would retire. Move to a small coastal fishing village where you would sleep late, fish a little, play with your kids, take siestas with your wife, and stroll to the village in the evenings where you could sip wine and play your guitar with your amigos."

[*Source:* "The Mexican Fisherman" story came from a short story, *Anekdote zur Senkung der Arbeitsmoral* ("Anecdote Concerning the Lowering of Productivity"), published by a German writer, Heinrich Böll, in 1963.]

Here's to money-minded families everywhere! May you and your children save well, spend well, share well, invest well, and live well.

15

Let's Recap

The Top Financial Wellness Practices:
- Financial socialization is a learned process of acquiring knowledge and developing skills. Use this book to acquire the knowledge to develop new skills for yourself and your family.
- Financial wellbeing can be learned and practiced like any other life skill.
- Conscious spending and saving will not only help you meet your financial goals, it will demonstrate the same skills for your children.
- Find teachable moments about your child's favorite store to talk about budgeting to buy their favorite things.
- Explain to your child how a credit card works and why you are using it.
- When possible, have your child pay or participate in a spending decision.
- Habits are the strongest foundation for healthy financial wellness.
- Take the money personality quiz to understand your starting point (https://ig.ft .com/sites/quiz/psychology-of-money/).
- Evaluate your decisions in light of your newfound personality.
- Embrace your family's money personality and understand the positive and negative lessons you can learn from it.
- Money is a leading cause of stress, but try to use deliberate thinking in order to impact positive financial behaviors and lead to decreased anxiety about financial matters.
- Understand how your generation influenced your money mindset and how your child's generation is influencing theirs.
- Money is just a thing; never make the mistake of giving it your power.
- Think in terms of your personal economy.
- Consider: What are you willing to trade your life energy for?
- Learning takes place best when people are active, engaged, social, and building meaningful connections. Create financial learning opportunities for your children that allow them to be active, not passive, participants in the process.

- Just like when setting goals for life, setting goals for money requires you to be mindful and deliberate.
- Take the time to exercise Goal Planning with a Purpose. Walk through the process for both yourself and your child. Follow through and evaluate your and their success.
- Remind your children: Abundance is within you, *not* in things.
- Teach your children to put time and space between their purchases; exercise Advanced Purchase Planning; this will help to eliminate the instant gratification sickness we have.
- Pay yourself first.
- Make saving automatic.
- Introduce the concept of a budget to your child as soon as they begin to spend.
- When your child is faced with taking on debt, calculate what they can actually afford and the length of time they will carry the debt.
- Limit student loan debt to 10% or less of your after-tax monthly income.
- Richness comes from your soul, spirit, character, and values.
- Mindful spending is spending that aligns with your values; try the exercise Can Money Make you Happy? with your child.
- Spend less, research more.
- Earning money is the key to success.
- Make sure your children understand how to earn and the implications of taxes and other expenses for their paycheck.
- Before making a major purchase, have your children do the research to understand what they truly can afford.
- Find your passion and use your personal resources to help fulfill it.
- Philanthropy provides a wonderful platform for educating the next generation as to family dynamics, the importance of giving money away, and the role of outside advisors.
- What you appreciate, appreciates.
- Give with intention and do your research.
- Investing should not be a short-term game, but rather a long-term journey.
- Investing is necessary to building wealth.
- Introduce your children to investing once their savings bucket is full; have them research and find stocks to buy.
- Small investments at a young age will reduce intimidation and will teach the basics of risk and reward to your child.
- At least annually, review your account statements with your child.
- Discuss protecting your most precious assets with the proper insurance.

And finally:
- *Have fun!*

Additional Resources

Books

Elementary School

A Chair for My Mother
Written by: Vera B. Williams
Illustrated by: Vera B. Williams
The Berenstain Bears' Trouble with Money
Written by: Stan Berenstain, Jan Berenstain
Lemonade in Winter
Written by: Emily Jenkins
Illustrated by: G. Brian Karas
A Dollar for Penny
Written by: Julie Glass
Illustrated by: Joy Allen
The Girl and the Bicycle
Written by: Mark Pett
Illustrated by: Mark Pett
Rickshaw Girl
Written by: Mitali Perkins
Illustrated by: Jamie Hogan

Middle School

How Ella Grew an Electric Guitar
Written by: Ellen Neuborne, Orly Sade
The Everything Kids' Money Book
Written by: Brette McWhorter Sember
Better Than a Lemonade Stand!: Small Business Ideas for Kids
Written by: Daryl Bernstein
The Know-Nonsense Guide to Money: An Awesomely Fun Guide to the World of Finance!
Written by: Heidi Fiedler
Illustrated by: Brendan Kearney
A Smart Girl's Guide: Money
Written by: Nancy Holyoke
How to Turn $100 into $1,000,000: Earn! Save! Invest!
Written by: James McKenna, Jeannine Glista, Matt Fontaine

High School

The Motley Fool Investment Guide for Teens: 8 Steps to Having More Money Than Your Parents Ever Dreamed Of
Written by: David Gardner, Tom Gardner, Selena Maranjian
The Young Entrepreneur's Guide to Starting a Business: Turn Your Ideas Into Money!
Written by: Steve Mariotti
The Richest Man in Babylon
Written by: George S. Clason

Toy Learning

Melissa and Doug Play Money
Manufacturer: Melissa and Doug
Pretend and Play Calculator Cash Register
Manufacturer: Learning Resources Inc.
Pretend and Play Checkbook with Calculator
Manufacturer: Learning Resources
Moonjar Three-Part Moneybox
Smart Pig Trio Bank
Manufacturer: Giantsuper
Time and Money Flash Cards
Manufacturer: Brighter Child
Cash 'n' Carry Wallet
Manufacturer: Learning Resources
Money Bags: A Coin Value Game
Manufacturer: Learning Resources
Loose Change
Manufacturer: MindWare
Moneywise Kids
Manufacturer: TaliCor
The Game of Life and Monopoly

Apps

Elementary

Savings Spree
Renegade Buggies
Bankaroo

Green$treets
Piggy Bot

Middle School and Older

Wally and Acorns—to keep up to date with new games, books and apps the websites Nerd Wallet and Motley Fool are great resources.
Greenlight
Family Zoo
Mint
YNAB

Index